# THE JEWISH FAMILY

# THE JEWISH FAMILY

*Authority and Tradition
in Modern Perspective*
**Norman Linzer**, *Ph.D.*

*Wurzweiler School of Social Work
Yeshiva University, New York*

**HUMAN SCIENCES PRESS, INC.**
*72 FIFTH AVENUE,
NEW YORK, N.Y. 10011*

Printed in the United States of America
987654321


**Library of Congress Cataloging in Publication Data**

Linzer, Norman.
  The Jewish family.

  Bibliography
  Includes index.
  1. Jewish families.   I. Titles.
HQ525.J4L56          1983          306.8'5'088296          83-12775
ISBN 0-89885-149-1
ISBN 0-89885-191-2 (pbk.)

*To my wife, Diane*
*and my children,*
*Moshe, Dov, Menachem*
*and Michal*

# CONTENTS

# FOREWORD

My acquaintance with Norman Linzer, who is an ordained rabbi as well as professor of social work at Yeshiva University, goes back to our days as fellow-students of Rabbi Joseph B. Soloveitchik. Therefore, when he decided to spend a sabbatical year with us at the Shalom Hartman Institute in Jerusalem, it was both a personal pleasure and a source of intellectual stimulation to us all. During that year we were privileged to witness and participate in the profound spiritual struggle out of which the present book on the Jewish family was born.

Since Professor Linzer employs traditional Jewish perspectives to illuminate the situation of the modern Jewish family, a few remarks about those perspectives can provide a context for understanding the importance of his work.

To begin with, the Jewish community is the central frame of reference for the development of the Judaic world view. *Halakhah* ( Jewish jurisprudence) translates the consciousness of God within the social, political, and economic structures of the community. The Sinai covenant was made with a chosen people, not with chosen individuals. In Judaism, therefore, election is not an individualistic but a political concept. Judaism is concerned with providing a system of meaning for the life of a community, rather than with offering salvation for

9

the individual human soul. The collective structure of human life is challenged to embody the sovereignty of God. "You shall be a holy people" is a call to a political action in which limits are placed upon the absolute sovereignty of human institutions over human beings. The kingdom of God is not merely an eschatological category, but above all a normative demand to be realized in the everyday existence of the community.

There is a profound statement in the Jerusalem Talmud according to which slaves are exempt from the commandment of reciting the *Shema Yisrael,* because the latter declares the unity and sovereignty of God in history, whereas they are subject to the manipulation and authority of human masters. Only one who is free from human exploitation can fully realize the command to acknowledge the sovereignty of God. Pronouncing the *Shema,* the basic Jewish declaration of faith, is not an inward performance unrelated to the individual's social and economic status in the community. That declaration of faith must have implications for the day in which the Jew builds his political frames of reference. It is in this sense that the community lies at the heart of the Judaic faith experience.

Peoplehood, community, land, covenant are all social and political categories. From a biblical perspective, Judaism is inconceivable outside the life of the community. The Promised Land is essential to covenantal consciousness because it was only within the geographical context of the land that the Jewish community could fully realize its spiritual aspirations. A religion whose primary aim is individual salvation on the other hand, does not essentially require a particular geographic location to structure the aspiration of realizing the life of faith. Thus the centrality of the land in Judaism is not a vestige of primitive tribalism or land mysticism, but derives from awareness that covenantal consciousness and the striving to acknowledge the kingdom of God must be mirrored in the political structure of the community.

When the Jewish people lost its land and went into *galut* (exile), Judaism could no longer be fully realized in everyday life. Accordingly, it acquired a provisional character, which remained such despite the many centuries for which *galut* lasted. *Galut* spirituality was regarded by the Talmud as incomplete, in a deeper sense, as antithetical to the ultimate spirit of Judaism. *Galut* was conceived in the categories of mourning, of alienation, of being cut off from the full source of life. A constant longing was felt in *galut* Judaism, the longing of the Jew to anchor temporal existence in a larger frame of reference; yet the suffering of the Jewish people never shifted the focus of that longing from the lost land to the hope for eternal life. The hope for immortality is not central to the spiritual drama of Judaism, nor is the eschatological hope for redemption and a final resolution of human suffering. Judaism stands or falls on its ability to sanctify the everyday life of society. It is within the economic, social, and political spheres of society that the Judaic faith demands to be evaluated.

Given, therefore, the centrality of the community as distinct from the individual, one can appreciate the role of the family within the Judaic tradition. The family is the social institution that brings the individual into the community. The family mediates the larger communal memories. Parents within the Judaic tradition, as Norman Linzer fully recognizes, tell stories whereby the child is linked to a larger drama that overcomes the loneliness of the biological individual and turns him or her into a member of a historical covenantal community. Human consciousness becomes historical when families mediate a historical drama. This is why the holiday of Passover, which celebrates the birth of the community, is celebrated within the context of the family. In a symbolic sense, parents feed their children the bread of slavery and the longing for freedom. They recite together the Passover *haggadah*, the story of how the Hebrew slaves were led out of Egypt. They create a living drama in which the present is saturated with the pilgrimage of a people on their way to attaining full national political existence. In the *galut* context, the narration was a reaffirmation of the aspiration to return to the land and to political independence. The Passover night of storytelling ends with the proclamation of the centrality of Jerusalem—"Next year in Jerusalem."

Jerusalem is not a synagogue, nor is it a church nor a frame of reference for lonely souls who seek eternity and freedom from death. Jerusalem is a city in which a community builds its present reality in interaction with the covenant of Sinai. It is a city that invites the prophetic message to enter modernity, that teaches ahistorical, technological man that we have no future if we have no anchor nor roots in our historic past. Ending the Passover seder with "Next year in Jerusalem" reminds Jews throughout the Diaspora that fundamentally Judaism is a collective drama, to be realized within the temporal framework of history.

It is, I believe, not accidental that Norman Linzer's important work on the family was written during his sabbatical year in Jerusalem. His serious struggle with rehabilitating the role of the Jewish family in modernity was nourished by the intellectual and spiritual forces found within this city. The impact of the centrality of Israel in Jewish consciousness initiated a spiritual upheaval in Norman Linzer's work. He fully discerned that Judaism is not a *galut* experience in which one focuses exclusively on the minutiae of ritual. Notwithstanding the indispensability of symbolic ritual, one must recognize that reborn Israel is a call to focus on new spiritual categories that deal with larger political and social issues.

Linzer is concerned with rehabilitating the significance of the family in modernity. His serious attempt to show how the Judaic tradition offers ways in which to make the family a vital and viable institution in modern life deserves serious consideration. He is breaking new ground in the way he deals with Judaic material. Linzer's work creates an interdisciplinary frame of reference in which social values, political thought, and the *Halakhah* and *Aggadah* interweave in a unified discussion. He does not employ Jewish tradition as an authoritarian frame of reference, but is prepared to expose the classical material of Judaism to the searching analysis of modern categories of thought. One may take issue with details of his approach and conclusions, but one cannot escape his intellectual integrity and spiritual earnestness.

It is my fervent hope that Norman Linzer's work will find a broad audience, and that discussion on the political and social implications of the family will become a central concern of those involved in Judaic thought. His work should prove helpful to all who wrestle with the problem of autonomy and authority and the use and abuse of dependency. Linzer has shown in his book that these important psychological and political categories are not unfamiliar to *Halakhah*, but are essential in making sense of Judaism as a way of life.

I am happy that Jerusalem, and specifically the community in our Institute, could provoke a serious social scientist to grapple with a crucial Jewish political question, the role and significance of the family.

David Hartman, Ph.D.
Director, Shalom Hartman Institute
Jerusalem

# INTRODUCTION

This book is the product of a year's study and research at the Shalom Hartman Institute for Advanced Judaic Studies in Jerusalem. It was conceived while I was on a leave of absence following a Sabbatical from the Wurzweiler School of Social Work of Yeshiva University. Some of the ideas were tested in one of my courses at the Bar Ilan University School of Social Work, where I taught for two years.

The Institute comprises 25 postdoctoral scholars, educators, communal leaders, and university students, both men and women, who reflect the religious diversity that exists in contemporary Jewish life. Their knowledge of Judaism is wide-ranging, encompassing the Bible, Talmud, Midrash, Jewish philosophy and ethics.

My approach to the subject matter of this book and my growth through the research and writing process evolved during the learning experience of this year. It was in the Institute's *Beit Midrash*—study hall—that the inspiration to pursue the theme and contents of the book emerged.

The year at the Institute was like no other in my educational biography. When a new experience and status are deeply meaningful to a person, one tends to redefine one's past, so that it pales in comparison with the current life situation. My previous study of Judaism was textually based, exploring and analyzing the world of the commentaries, their differences, and their ways of interpretation. The goal in each class was to cover 20 to 30 pages of the Talmudic tractate and to derive what one could of the subjects discussed in those pages, regardless of their practicality to contemporary life. As I contemplated the intricacies of the Talmudic mind and reasoning, I found this study to be intellectually stimulating. As a result of my experience at the Institute, I have redefined my previous Jewish education as having been limited and confining, though it certainly didn't seem that way at the time. Yet I now know that it could have been different, and this awareness derived from my exposure to the educational philosophy and methodology of the Institute.

The Institute's ethos is based on a unique characteristic: a deep commitment to Judaism, and intellectual openness. These attitudes are normally viewed as incompatible, for it seems contradictory to be both committed to the legal tradition and yet be open to difference. But it is this feature of the Institute that contributes to the dynamic tension and growth potential inherent in the learning process. There is no appeal to authority and no respect of persons; one has to be convinced through reason. Students present multiple points of view on the same issue and support their claims through rigorous analytic skill.

The learning atmosphere is one of free inquiry: any questions may be asked, even though they touch upon the basic articles of faith. We probe into the meanings of the classical sources, beginning with the Bible and its commentaries, moving on to the Prophets and their commentaries, and only then arriving at the Talmudic text with its commentaries. All along this process, the individual's own perspective is encouraged prior to the commentaries' interpretations. What do I think about this text?—what does it say to me?—what are the difficulties inherent in its syntax?—how do I interpret it?—what is its application to the contemporary situation? These are some of the questions asked as a subject is studied.

The spirit of free inquiry and individual initiative brought a freshness to Talmud study that I had never experienced before. I was encouraged to use my own powers of reasoning and analysis, before being influenced by the traditional commentaries to think in their prescribed ways. Upon learning their views, I was then able to assess the similarities and differences in our perspectives. The opportunities for the student's own interpretations are available due to the fact that the Sages themselves did not generally provide the conceptual framework for their discussions; they tended to support their arguments from the minutiae of the biblical syntax. Conceptualizations were usually reserved for the great rabbis and commentators. At the Institute, however, students were encouraged to do this by asking, "What are they really arguing about; what is the Talmud trying to say?" The latter is the primary research question that motivates learning and inquiry.

The student attempts to understand the text in its context and language, and to utilize a personal conceptual orientation to make it intelligible to the modern way of thinking. Thus, such intellectual disciplines as philosophy, political science, sociology, psychology, and law are common frames of reference from which textual analysis and inferences are made. I was encouraged to utilize my background in sociology as a tool for interpreting the ideas behind the text. The goal was to penetrate the Talmudic mind and thereby gain access to the profundity and complexity of Judaic thought.

The Institute's central methodological question is: how to move from the legal tradition with its formal, legal categories to experiences that reflect human values and meanings, and then to an understanding of these experiences based upon modern scientific theories of human functioning. There is a continuous effort to translate the theological into the human, to comprehend God's expectations for man, to emphasize the meaning of the human in the covenantal encounter with the Divine. There are, therefore, two languages: the language of the tradition with its theological connotations, and the language of modernity with its secular orientation. Both languages are utilized in order to strengthen one's commitment to the tradition, and through intellectual openness, to appreciate the tradition's diversity and its parallels in the pluralism of modern thought. The theme of study was Jewish political philosophy. We probed the Sages' perspectives on the establishment of governing bodies and their relationship with the governed, and the dynamics and roles of political leadership. Throughout the study of each figure of political import—the king, the sage, the prophet, and even the community—the major theme was political authority, its sources, its dynamics in social relationships, its role in maintaining social order, and other functions. The purpose of studying this subject was to seek ways of utilizing Jewish conceptions of political processes, in order to ultimately suggest changes in political institutions in the State of Israel to conform to Torah values and prescriptions. In short, it was to determine the viability of the Jewish political state in modern times.

The authority theme dominated my consciousness throughout the year. It became the center of my cognitive concern, with its components reaching into diverse areas of human functioning, but particularly in two of my interests: the family, and social work. The issue of authority is central in the relationship between parents and children, and between the social worker and the client. In looking at the family, we are not only concerned with the parents' authority, but also with its impact on the independent strivings of children. The social worker, too, who aims to fashion a professional relationship with the client by the constructive use of professional authority, is primarily concerned with freeing the client from subservience to the "authority" of traditional modes of behavior and from dependence on the social worker for guidance and direction.

In our study of political and religious institutions, the relationship between their authority and traditions, and the autonomy of the individual, was constantly posed as central to an understanding of the essence of Jewish thought. What role is there for the individual in the face of the massive weight of institutionalized authority? Is he or she permitted to disagree and argue with the representatives of the system? Does halakhic—Jewish legal—authority tolerate and even encourage individual difference and initiative? What sanction is given by Jewish law to intellectually honest disagreements? Essentially, the question that is being posed concerns the viability of religious pluralism in the Jewish community. The outcome of this year's study has been a qualified "yes" answer. It depends upon which trends of interpretation one chooses to emphasize within the divergent points of view, expressed in the classical sources of Jewish tradition. This is an important, if not yet fully developed, area for further research.

The relationship between the authority of the tradition and the autonomy of the individual serves as the philosophical framework of this book. It is closely related to both the traditional and the modern Jewish family because the essence of children's growth and parents' self-development lies in the encounter of parental authority with child independence, and in their underlying values. My goal was to discover in the Jewish sources a framework from which to understand this issue in the contemporary Jewish family. Along the way, additional interests were stimulated, so that the final product contains a perspective from Jewish tradition on some central themes in modern Jewish family life.

The view from the tradition is addressed to both traditional and non-traditional Jews. It is the thesis of this book that Jewish tradition speaks to moderns even as it did to ancients, that it provides guidance and frames of reference for all Jews. One need not believe in the divine origin of the

*Halakhah* to derive principles for family life. These are available for study and reflection, and application to one's immediate experience. Modern Jews of various ideological persuasions are invited to become acquainted with the values and norms of Jewish family life as portrayed in the tradition, and to select for implementation those that address their interests and needs most directly.

The perspective is conceptual, not programmatic, as I leave it for parents and for those actively engaged in service to Jewish families to translate these approaches into concrete programs. I sincerely believe that programs and techniques alone will not solve the many difficult problems facing Jewish families in the modern world; rather, parents and professionals require a Jewish philosophical perspective to help them conceptualize the stresses and forces impinging on the family. Knowledge and understanding could then lead to action.

Because traditional Jewish society was patriarchal and the classical Judaic sources were addressed mainly to families composed of two parents and their children, this book, which distills those sources and attempts to translate them into modern categories, focuses on the intact nuclear Jewish family. The underlying assumption is that the father and mother are present in the home, want to fulfull their roles as parents, and not escape the responsibilities that these roles entail. In addition, they are not merely satisfied with the status quo, but continually strive to improve their parental functioning.

I am aware of the possible criticism regarding the book's focus on this type of family structure and its exclusion of an increasingly large percentage of single-parent families, and reconstituted families. In both these family constellations, the authority dimension is weakend; in the single-parent family it is reduced and in the reconstituted family it is diffused. Thus, these families need to accommodate to their altered forms and raise children in nonconformity with traditional life styles. This departure, however, does not compromise the research findings, for such research sheds light on the goals, values, and functions of Jewish families in general. Though their social structures differ, modern families can still derive deeper insights and understanding of their goals, values, and functions from their predecessors. Parents are encouraged to make connections to their own family situations. Professionals, too, are urged to draw their own inferences from the material in order to serve their clients with more insight.

As in all research endeavors, this one does not lay claim to the resolution of the problems of its subject—the modern Jewish family. There are multiple problems and diverse families, and no one treatise can hope to address itself to all of them. I have, therefore, attempted to explore what I deem to be the central issue confronting Jewish families today—the decline of authority and the ascendance of individualism as primary social values. This issue had been addressed peripherally in my previous books, *The Jewish Family* and *The Nature of Man in Judaism and Social Work,* but here it is the central theme.

The two previous books were the products of my teaching the *Jewish Social Philosophy* course at the Wurzweiler School of Social Work of Yeshiva University over many years. In *The Jewish Family,* I selected topics that dealt with husband-wife relationships, such as marriage, sexuality, birth control, abortion, and divorce; topics were also focused on parents and children, which included adoption, foster care, drugs, holocaust survivors, and the aged. The book presented halakhic sources on these topics as background for a discussion of cases from the family and child welfare agencies affiliated with the Federation of Jewish Philanthropies of New York. My aim was to provide social workers with a Jewish perspective on various aspects of family life in order to sensitize them to the Jewish dimension in their professional work.

As *The Jewish Family* dealt with practical issues in social work practice, *The Nature of Man in Judaism and Social Work* was primarily philosophically oriented. Topics included time, the dual nature of man, good and evil, holocaust survivors, sin and repentance, public and private spheres of reality, and the Jewish family. My purpose was to educate Jewish social workers in philosophical speculations on human beings and their social functioning, and how human existence is conceived by Judaism as a religion and social work as a profession. In those books, I presented my approach to the resolution of the disparities between Judaism and social work. I now realize that my answers may not really work for others; they are not even satisfactory for me because the issues are too complex and changing to be constrained within definitive explications. Therefore in this book I have desisted from making the connections between religion and the profession and instead free the reader to infer them. The reader's own discoveries will thus be more exciting through self-motivated initiative. I do share my inclinations and leanings, but I do not try to resolve the issues for practice. I leave it to practitioners in various helping disciplines to translate them into their own professional frameworks. I also encourage parents to draw implications for their own families, with their unique constellation of roles, statuses, values, and purposes.

Most of the chapters in this book were first presented as lectures at various forums in Israel. The ensuing discussions enriched my understanding of the issues and many of the ideas were subsequently incorported.

Chapter I, *Traditional Authority and Individual Autonomy: A Jewish Perspective on Modernity,* sets forth the theme of the book. It is a concentrated integration of the year's study at the Shalom Hartman Institute. It describes my efforts at understanding the relationship between the authority of tradition and its institutions, and the individual's striving for self-assertion. An integrative model is proposed for the modern Jew, and a case from the Jewish classical tradition highlights this conflict.

Chapter II, *Authority and Independence in Jewish Family Relationships,* follows naturally from chapter I. It translates the central issue into the core of the family experience, and sets the theme for all subsequent discussions. The ideas of this chapter were first presented at an Oneg Shabbat forum in Kibbutz Lavie. Research concentrated on the traditional commentaries' discussion of the two biblical verses denoting filial responsibility to parents. Upon ordering the data, I discovered a model for Jewish family relationships. Parents are seen by the Sages as symbols but also as real people, and the relationships between parents and children are finely honed by the fulfillment of their mutual obligations and needs. The emergent model of authority-independence recognizes the inevitability of tension between these obligations and needs, and offers a means for its reduction through mutual interdependence.

Chapter III, *Models of Authority-Independence Relationships in the Modern Jewish Family*, reviews the ideal-typical model from Jewish tradition and discusses its inapplicability to the contemporary situation. The discovery that the traditional model was not based in Jewish historical reality was made during its presentation to an adult study group affiliated with the Institute. Instead, three models are proposed, which are represented by different segments of the Jewish community. The alternate models, in conversation with the traditional one, derive from my acquaintance with the diversity of life styles and structures in the contemporary Jewish family.

Chapter IV, *The Passage from Childhood to Adulthood*, focuses on the critical stage of the authority-independence issue: adolescence. The theme of the chapter, though, is not on the parent-child conflict, but on a comparison of Judaic, anthropological, and psychological knowledge of this stage of life. The study was motivated by the invitation to speak to high school teachers in Kiryat Shemona and Emek Hayarden, as part of the Institute's service to educational institutions. I was curious about Judaism's attitude toward adolescence, the stages of childhood, the struggles that adolescents face in growing up, and the essential meaning of the rite of passage—*bar-mitzvah*. Insights are offered for understanding the modern Jewish adolescent whose developmental tasks are both similar to and different from those of his predecessor.

Chapter V, *Combating Narcissism in the Jewish Family*, is the only chapter which was not presented before an audience in Israel. It is a revision of my article entitled, *The Modern Jew and the Human Condition: The Impact of Tradition and Secularism*, in the Spring 1980 issue of the *Journal of Jewish Communal Service*. The revision was motivated by two factors: dissatisfaction with the form and content of the article, and a different conception of God's revelation to man which serves as a model for the individual's relationship to other human beings. The contrast between Soloveitchik's "self-renunciation" approach and Hartman's "self-transcendence" approach became boldly clear. These comprise two diverse proposals for combating narcissism in the modern Jewish family.

Narcissism is defined as exaggerated individualism, a deification of the self which does not honor the status of authority figures. Such behavior creates conflict in the family and breeds its dissolution. The two Jewish approaches are ideological because they deal with the value orientations in the family. The professional is advised to encompass the family as a unit in the clinical purview and services, in preference to the treatment of its individual members, in order to help them combat narcissistic tendencies.

Chapter VI, *The Faith and Pathology of Holocaust Survivor Families*, was adapted from an address at the Community Mental Health Center in Safed. The faith issue is prominent among survivors, and the pathology inheres in the relationship between survivors and their children. Faith was a concern of practically all survivors, regardless of the degree of their faith and religious observance prior to the holocaust. The pathology is complex and multifaceted: its major focus is on the conflict between second generation children's need to separate from their parents and become autonomous adults, and their parents' felt need to protect them from real and imagined dangers and to continue to control their lives. Thus this chapter is a case illustration of a particular type of Jewish family where the authority-independence issue is exaggerated.

Chapter VII, *Toward a Modern Family Portrait*, is the concluding chapter in which the major themes of the book are reviewed. It points toward the development of approaches and services for the Jewish family in the Jewish community. Parents are encouraged to study Jewish texts and to experience Jewish life intensely in social settings in order to integrate Jewish tradition with their modern consciousness. Professionals are encouraged to develop a vision of Jewish family life, along with a philosophy of the meaning and value of family life for Jews. They need to help families in three dimensions—the educational, the experiential, and the social—which will enable them to strengthen their ties to each other and grow together.

The experience of living in Israel has contributed to the inspiration for writing this book. As a Jew who lived comfortably in the United States, I had never really conceived of Israel as a viable option. It was the place one visited to be reaffirmed as a Jew and to renew one's acquaintances with Jewish history. But after having lived here for 2 years, this attitude has undergone radical change. Israel seems to be an option no longer, but a vital necessity. It beckons committed Jews to fashion a new society, to become part of a transcendent entity. It is a reality that calls for the Jew's reach to exceed his grasp. Israel offers the opportunity to build a new nation based on Jewish values, to fashion a modern Jewish state with all its complications, struggles, and uncertainty.

For the first time I understand the concept of redemption. Redemption from the Diaspora means the ascension to a more spiritual plane of existence, and the cleansing of the taint of assimilation even for the imperfect purity of a heterogeneous

Jewish society. One is redeemed when one's Jewish memory is located in the geography of Jewish history. One feels oneself to be part of the Jewish past not through a leap of imagination, but through the recall of the eye's vision. Anywhere one stands in Israel, and particularly in Jerusalem, one can hear Abraham's footsteps traversing the land, the thunder of Joshua's armies, the sweet strings of David's harp, the music of Temple celebrations.

Redemption is not just an aesthetic, emotional experience; it also obligates. Redemption demands that each Jew contribute to the building of the society, to the sharing of talents, to strengthening the indivisible bonds between Jew and Jew, and to forging the unity of the nation. Redemption requires the execution of the creative impulse in eliminating poverty, fostering full employment, raising educational standards, building bridges between the religious and the non-religious, providing food, clothing, and shelter for an entire population. Living in Israel provides the religious supports for the creative gesture. It reinforces the drive to excel, to create, and to express one's deepest emotions and yearnings. In the experience of redemption, one is transplanted to a more spiritual level of existence. One's soul is enflamed with love for all Jews, love for the land, love for the Torah, and love for God.

I am deeply indebted to David Hartman who believed in the possibility of my continued intellectual and spiritual growth. I am grateful to Tzvi Marx who read the entire manuscript and helped me to sharpen my arguments and literary style, and to my colleagues at the Institute whose brilliance and insights taught me a new way to study and analyze Jewish texts. Hagi Ben-Artzi, my study partner, was a constant source of intellectual challenge. Florence Mittwoch supported me throughout two years of teaching at Bar Ilan with her warmth and encouragement. Rifka Ausubel Danzig and Charles S.

Levy of Wurzweiler made helpful suggestions. Ruth Sherer typed the manuscript quickly and impeccably. And I wish to sincerely thank my wife Diane, and children, Moshe, Dov, Menachem, and Michal for their patience in putting up with my determination to bring this project to fruition.

Norman Linzer
Jerusalem

# Chapter 1

# TRADITIONAL AUTHORITY AND INDIVIDUAL AUTONOMY:

# A JEWISH PERSPECTIVE ON MODERNITY

He was being taken out to be executed for a hideous crime. There was absolutely no doubt in the court's mind that he was guilty. Though the decision was painful and deeply disturbing to the justices, they had arrived at a guilty verdict after very careful investigation and much deliberation. Some minor opposition within their ranks that noted the doubtful veracity of the witnesses' testimony was overruled by the majority, citing the weight of the evidence against the defendant. He was clearly a condemned man, doomed imminently to die.

When he was about 10 feet away from the execution site, the court representatives accompanying him suggest that he confess to the crimes he had committed, so that he will die in a state of purity and be eligible for a heavenly reward. He claims that he cannot recall other crimes, and becomes agitated at the prospect of his impending end. He begins to sob and choke. They proceed to tell him what to say and he repeats the words,

"May my death be an expiation for all my sins," but he doesn't feel the sentiment. He is preoccupied with himself and cannot relate to anyone or anything.

Then, in a burst of daring and impulse, he shouts: "But I'm innocent; you're killing an innocent man; I'm a victim of false evidence!" The men are astounded. They did not expect this outburst; their composure is ruffled and they begin to argue with him. Finally one of them says, "Look, it's too late now, but we'll permit you to change the wording in the confession to exclude this particular crime." The other retorts, "No. How could you do this? The consequences would be very serious. Everyone, including a person who is really guilty, would say this in order to clear himself in people's eyes and the court would acquire a bad reputation. We can't let him get away with a public expression of innocence." Thereupon the first speaker bows to the persuasive argument of the second and slams the lid on the condemned man's wish to assert his individuality for the last time.

This story is a reconstruction of a procedure cited in the Talmud (Sanhedrin 43b). The Talmud discusses the confession that the court seeks to extract from the condemned to bring him to a state of *teshuvah*—repentance—before his death, and to preserve the integrity of the court's authority. The disagreement between the court's representatives dramatizes the dispute between R. Judah and the Sages regarding the individual's right publicly to proclaim his innocence, thereby undermining the legitimacy of the court's authority. Though the legal decision favors the Sages' opinion, R. Judah's opinion symbolizes the support which the rabbis gave to the individual to express his difference with, and opposition to, the central authority system in the Jewish community when he thought it erred in its judgment.

The story sets the theme of this chapter, which will discuss 1) perspectives on tradition and authority; 2) attitudes toward religious tradition in a secular society; 3) a particular Jewish approach to bridge the gap between tradition and modernity; and 4) classical sources of rabbinic authority and individual autonomy. After a case presentation from the Talmud which illustrates the conflict between rabbinic authority and individual autonomy, implications are drawn for the helping professions.

In the presentation of the theme, two levels of interaction between traditional authority and individual autonomy will be interwoven: the intellectual and the behavioral. On both the intellectual and behavioral levels, the question arises as to whether the central authority system sanctions the individual's disagreement. As exemplified in the Talmudic story, intellectual deviation is sanctioned, at least by a minority opinion, but behaviorally, deviation is unacceptable. The implications of this division for modern Jews will be explored at the end of the chapter.

## PERSPECTIVES ON TRADITION AND AUTHORITY

The authority of tradition, according to Weber (1947), is based on a people's belief in the legitimacy and sanctity of what has always existed (pp. 130-1). The system of order continues to be binding so long as belief in the legitimacy of the tradition is maintained. Attitudes toward change in laws and customs are psychologically inhibited, lest severe penalties ensue. Change emerges from two sources: prophetic pronouncements, "It is written...but I say unto you..." or from "the fiction" that the "new" laws had actually once been in force but had fallen into disuse, and only now are being brought back to their rightful position of authority. Thus, an important consequence of traditional authority is that there can be no such thing as new legislation.

In a society based on traditional authority, "obedience is not owed to enacted rules, but to the person who occupies a position of authority by tradition or who has been chosen for

such a position on a traditional basis (p.328)." Weber distinguishes between obedience to rules and obedience to people
who embody the rules. The rules require explication and application to the realities of everyday life. The group of scholars
and elders who have studied the rules and lived the tradition is
vested with the authority. The source of their authority is not
inherent in themselves but derives from the tradition which
they have internalized and transmitted to the people.

Weber relegates traditional authority to an irrational status, in contrast to rational-legal authority which is based on
reason and law. It is irrational because the force of the tradition
defies logical changes in its rules. The answer to the question,
"Why must we do it this way?" is, "Because we've always
done it this way." The documents of tradition—its prece-
dents—permit only its continued development within the
framework of what was, but not serious questioning,
disagreement, nor radical change.

Weber's contrast of reason with authority implied that the
methods of reason were scientific, as compared with the methods of authority, which were based upon revelation or irrational belief. Weber did not conceive the possibility that both tradition and authority might themselves be rational.

Arendt (1966) appears to support Weber's position. In her
discussion of the nature of authority, she states what it is not,
and then traces its origins back to Greek and Roman times.
Authority is not coercion by force or persuasion through arguments. "The authoritarian relation between the one who commands and the one who obeys rests neither on common reason
nor on the power of the one who commands; what they have in
common is the hierarchy itself, whose rightness and legitimacy
both recognize and where both have their predetermined stable
place (p.93)." Arendt claims that, to Plato and Aristotle,
authority derives from the structure of the relationship.

Plato sought a relationship in which the compelling element of authority lies in the relationship itself and precedes the

actual issuance of commands. For example, the patient became subject to the physician's authority when he fell ill, and not when he actually visited him. Here the source of authority does not lie in possession of the means of violence, in power, but is inherent in particular models of relationship. Aristotle maintained that authority does not derive from the superiority of the expert over the layperson but from natural inequality. It was inherent in the difference between young and old wherein some were destined to rule and others to be ruled. The actual term derives from the Latin *auctoritas,* to augment. Those in authority constantly augment the foundation of the society, namely its religion and tradition; they derive their authority from the authority of the founders which had its roots in the past.

The Romans bequeathed to future generations the interconnected trinity of religion, tradition, and authority as the essential foundation of the political realm. To Arendt, the "decline of the West" consists primarily in the decline of this trinity. In her conception, authority is basically irrational for it derives from, and is intertwined with, religion and tradition. Her question, "What is authority?" is essentially a search for the historical sources of political authority because it was not prevalent in Greek culture, whereas the Romans were able to establish the conception because of their political concerns.

The major source of political authority is the traditional base upon which it rests. Political tradition defines how rule in a society is conducted and how the ruled behave toward their rulers, how they elect and control them. Such tradition is embodied in customs, habits, and norms, which express the prevalent values and beliefs of the society. Hence, what is meant by tradition is its consensus by the group. Political tradition tends to resist political change, for it has existed for a long time. It insists upon a presumption in favor of what has endured. Traditionalism stresses and even glorifies the normative value of that which has been "in the time of our forefathers."

To the modern, scientific mind, this attitude to tradition is detrimental to human progress, for while it recognizes the value of tradition, it does not appreciate its limits. Tradition cannot address itself to the infinite variety of human experience, and social and ideological change in history. It should be seen not as a sure guide, but as a tentative guide for the discovery of new knowledge and new ways of dealing with old problems. All good science and scholarship is always based on tradition, as is all craftsmanship (Friedrich, 1972). No scientist begins *de novo*. A novice in science must master a body of established knowledge which is science's tradition, but innovation is then deliberately sought. Innovation is the means to a better understanding of a fundamentally unchanging reality. The more fundamental the innovation, the more esteemed the innovator once he or she has established its validity (Shils, 1981). The scientist's challenge is to reconcile the demands of the tradition with the impetus for innovation.

In the course of his discussion on scientific tradition, Popper (1965) suggests that there are two main attitudes possible toward tradition in general: to accept it as it is, uncritically, sometimes without even thinking about it, or to evaluate it critically.

Upon evaluating a tradition, we may accept it or reject it or perhaps compromise, but it will no longer be part of our taken-for-granted world. Once we begin to think about a tradition and decide whether we should accept or reject it, we free ourselves from its taboos. This is what Popper calls "second-order" tradition. First-order tradition is the handing down of a story from one generation to the next. Second-order tradition, bequeathed to us by the Greeks, is the critical discussion of the story or the myth. Second-order tradition characterizes modern science which grows primarily not through the accumulation of knowledge, but by revolutionary changes in scientific theories. It questions the validity of antecedent theory in the face of new discoveries, even as it builds upon that theory to move into new directions.

Tradition, whether in science or everyday life, plays a role similar to that of theories. Just as scientific theories help us to bring some order into the chaos in which we live so as to make it rationally predictable, so do traditions function in the same way. They help us to act rationally in response to behavior that is predictable because it has traditional antecedents. Traditions function similarly to institutions in that they both provide social order and predictability of behavior, but they refer to different facets of social life. Traditions describe ''a uniformity of people's attitudes, or ways of behavior, or aims or values, or tastes.'' Institutions are the norms or "*prime facie* social purposes (such as the propagation of knowledge, or protection from violence or starvation) (p. 132).'' Traditions are more than behavioral norms; they include attitudes and values. Institutions regulate behavior and prescribe social functions; they are primarily normative.

In sum, traditions possess authority because they derive from religion and/or wide acceptance by a group of people over the course of their common history. Traditions are adhered to because they contribute to the maintenance of social order and the predictability of behavior. They are indispensable for the continuity of social life. Traditions may be accepted and transmitted as received, ''first-order,'' or they may be evaluated critically, ''second-order.'' It may be broadly stated that pre-industrial societies tended toward a ''first-order'' attitude, whereas modern society tends toward a ''second-order'' attitude. A ''second-order'' attitude could lead to a rejection of the tradition.

## The Pluralization of Choices in Modern Society

In contrast to premodern societies, traditions and institutions in modern society are subject to greater rejection. Their taken-for-granted character has been eroded in the face of the pluralization of choices in the modern world. To insist that this is the way things are done because we've always done them that way is to open oneself to serious challenge to produce rational criteria for maintaining continuity in behavior. The reason for the pluralization of choices is the proliferation of institutions. Where there were one or two institutions in the past, there are now fifty. This means that there are many more programs for human activity, many of which open up numerous possibilities for individual choice.

Previously, socially defined reality had a high degree of objectivity. When one asked about the ways of the world, one was given a direct answer, to wit, "This is the way it is; there is no other way." In the modern world, this type of objectivity becomes eroded. Individuals are thrown back upon themselves to find some of their own answers to the perennial human questions whose answers are uncertain. The turning inward is what Berger (1979) calls "subjectivization."

> And all of this is very much connected with the transition from fate to choice: the taken-for-granted manner in which premodern institutions ordered human life is eroded. What previously was self-evident fact now becomes an occasion to choose. Fate does not require reflection; the individual who is compelled to make choices is also compelled to stop and think. The more choices, the more reflection. The individual who reflects inevitably becomes more conscious of himself, that is, he turns his attention from the objectively given outside world to his own subjectivity. As he does this, two things happen simultaneously: the outside world becomes more questionable, and his own inner world becomes more complex. Both of these things are unmistakable features of modern man (p. 22).

The turning inward occurs not only in the multiple realities of everyday life where institutions have proliferated, but also in the search for meaning in the religious experience. The pluralistic situation has created many more opportunities for choosing one's beliefs and rituals than heretofore. Since objective guidelines for choice do not exist, the individual must decide what to believe in, which ritual to practice, and how to do it. The field is open for choosing, experimenting, and discarding. Berger describes the "cognitive pressure" on the religious thinker, due to the pluralism and secularization that characterize modern society. He or she is pressured to deemphasize, if not to abandon altogether, the supernatural elements of the tradition. This is shared with all modern people—those still adhering to a religious tradition and those who no longer do so. Thus, modern man and woman find themselves more alone in the world as a result of the disappearance/denial of religious experience.

## THREE OPTIONS FOR THE RETENTION OF TRADITION

Berger posits three options for those who want to retain religious tradition: 1) to reaffirm the authority of the tradition in defiance of the challenges to it—the deductive option; 2) to try to secularize the tradition—the reductive option; 3) to try to uncover and retrieve the experiences embodied in the tradition—the inductive option.

In the deductive option, the individual reasserts the authority of the religious tradition in the face of modern secularity. Having restored the tradition to the status of a given, it is then possible to deduce religious affirmations at least more or less as was the norm in premodern times. God speaks to modern people as He did to the prophets. The message is the same for it is believed that the religious tradition is relevant for all times and places.

The tradition provides the individual with objective criteria of validity, thus preventing the relativization of personal existence in the midst of secular society. The disadvantage of this option is the difficulty of maintaining the subjective plausibility of such a procedure in the modern situation. The individual's realm of existence is narrow. One closes oneself off from thinking and learning about the modern world and participating in it; one sacrifices the intellect. One's attitude toward the tradition tends to be irrational, nonquestioning, and obedient. The psychological state is that of the obedient personality, dependent on the Law and its legitimate interpreters as guides for conduct, thus denying the integrity of one's own reason, doubts, and difference.

In the reductive option, the tradition is interpreted in modern secular terms by the individual who feels a compelling necessity to partake of the modern consciousness. This option appears to be more plausible for modern people. It entails a translation into modern categories of thought those religious traditions that speak of faith, ritual, and the spiritual. The faith images are demythologized and replaced with the vocabulary of social and behavioral science. Ethical as opposed to religious norms are elevated to primary status.

The tradition, taken as a whole, is conceived to be ana-chronistic, and inapplicable to modern concerns. The individual does not encounter it with respect and humility, as a body of laws, values and ideals that transcend the self. The person believes it is one's prerogative to manipulate and change it according to one's tastes and predilections. That which fits into one's image of secular life in a modern pluralistic society will be retained; that which reflects outdated concerns of bygone days will be rejected. The individual is the ultimate arbiter of the tradition's application to his or her life. The authority of modern thought or consciousness is substituted for the authority of the tradition. The individual considers modern consciousness to be the only criterion for the validity of religious reflection. The advantage of this approach is that it reduces cognitive dissonance between the claims of the tradition and the intellectual integrity of modern thought. Its disadvantage is the disappearance of the religious tradition in the course of its translation into secular language.

In the inductive option, the individual turns to personal experience as the ground of all religious affirmations. Human experience defines the phenomenon called religion. This experience can be described and analyzed; it begins with the human and proceeds to the metahuman, and not the reverse. The individual searches for similar experiences in religious history in order to validate their meaning and continuity for him or her self. There is a strong effort to traverse back into history to establish as accurately as possible the equivalent experience—how it really was—in those days. This provides an historical perspective for the immediate religious experience.

The emphasis in this option appears to be on the validation of the experience itself and not on the religious forms that emanate from it. The focus is on the experience and meaning of faith, and not on moral norms and religious rituals which derive from the faith experience. It uses the methods of the historian to uncover the human experiences that have become embodied in the religious traditions. The frame of mind engendered by this option is one which is unwilling to impose closure on the quest for religious truth by invoking any authority. Its advantage is the open-mindedness and freshness that usually comes from a nonauthoritarian approach to questions of truth. Its disadvantage is that open-mindedness tends to be linked to open-endedness, thus frustrating the deep religious hunger for certainty. "The substitution of hypothesis for proclamation is profoundly uncongenial to the religious temperament (Berger, p. 63)."

## THE INTEGRATIVE OPTION

There is a fourth option, the integrative, that goes beyond those enunciated by Berger. The central question addressed by the integrative option is: what is the relationship between tradition and reason? Can the individual, using reason, maintain a posture of critical loyalty to the tradition? The integrative option rejects the deductive option because it require total submission to the authority of traditional norms and the denial of reason in rethinking the tradition. It rejects the reductive option because it elevates reason above the tradition, accepts only those elements and norms which can be rationally deduced, and leaves no room for the experience of the numinous. It rejects the inductive option because its thrust is anthropocentric, and it circumscribes the legitimacy of the tradition only to those events which parallel contemporary human experience. Its concern is with the fit between the present and the past, without imagining that the past could transcend the present in wisdom and spirituality.

The integrative option "will not revel in norms that are not reasonable, nor consider the soul to be spiritually nurtured when it is obedient to that which it doesn't understand. On the contrary, actions which grow from understanding will be seen as the highest level of religious achievement (Hartman, 1976)." The spiritual values of the tradition become enhanced through the way of reason.

The starting point of the integrative option is in the classical sources of the religious tradition. Through the sources, it seeks to understand the purposes, functions, and structures of the society created by the religion's elders which managed to perpetuate itself through all vicissitudes of history. How difficult was this task, for it required that the ideological premises of human nature and social institutions be flexible enough to respond to the cultural challenges of the environment in each historical epoch. As additional layers of commentary and interpretation were appended to the tradition throughout the centuries, one could discern the rabbis' struggle to apprehend the past in the context of its time and place, and to apply the earlier teachings to changing circumstances without violating their authenticity.

In earlier times, the rabbis' attempts to apply the tradition to their own period appeared easier than today. Then, the language of study and the definition of reality were the same; the school, the home, and the immediate environment offered the same interpretation of reality, for there was a religious commitment to the authority of the tradition. Translation was done within a common universe of discourse. Now, the environment is pluralistic, as is consciousness. There is greater freedom of choice in matters of belief and morality. The language of everyday life is secular, devoid of religious intimations and content. The people who wrote the words of Jewish tradition did not interpret them for the modern reader. The complexities of modern issues were not formulated by the rabbinic scholars in the terminology in which they appear today. Considerable intellectual effort is required to recognize the concepts of the tradition, decipher their symbols, and then develop a language to understand them through the filter of current reality.

How did the rabbis translate the old tradition to fit new circumstances? What sources of authority did they use to make the changing reality intelligible, and introduce new norms acceptable to the people? They utilized the two sources of authority in Jewish tradition: the authority of Sinai, the laws which were received by Moses and transmitted down through the centuries on which there was no disagreement, and the authority of reason, the laws which they derived from the powers of reason and the application of the thirteen hermeneutic principles (Torat Kohanim, lev.1) on which there was disagreement. The authority of reason was not based on tradition but on the force and logic of argument. Where Sinaitic authority was inapplicable, the rabbis used reason and the logic of argument to fashion new norms and rescind old ones in guiding the community to function as an autonomous sociopolitical entity.

Supported by the rabbis' use of reason to meet the requirements of change and continuity in Jewish tradition, the integrative option stresses the use of reason by modern Jews in order to apply Jewish tradition to their life style in a secular society. It selects certain aspects of Berger's three options and discards the others. It accepts as essential the priority of commitment to Jewish tradition from the deductive option, the use of reason from the reductive option, and the significance of present experience from the inductive option. In the ensuing integration, the individual expresses a commitment to Jewish tradition but retains a posture of intellectual openness to its inherent diversity. One utilizes analytic tools to understand the tradition in its own terms, and then to translate it to one's realm of experience.

"To the degree that one can render one's tradition comprehensible to all people, to that degree one can argue that the way of reason and the way of tradition are harmonious (Hartman, p.19)." The legitimation of one's reason and the pluralization of one's actions are the keys for the modern Jew's connection to Jewish tradition. Once reason is sanctioned as a legitimate tool of interpretation, it supports the pluralistic approach toward the tradition. Reason presupposes disagreement and the pluralization of argument. Jewish tradition, replete with disputes among rabbis on various matters, respects and encourages the individual scholar's expression of difference, not only with the majority opinion, but even in the presence of the central authority system in the community (Sanhedrin 86b). Because of the absence of a central authority system in the modern Jewish community, there is ample room for diversity not only on the cognitive level but on the level of behavior as well.

The imposition of a uni-dimensional way of life is anathema to the integrative approach. It disdains unquestioning obedience to traditional authority and the false sense that there is only one way to truth. Instead, it encourages individualistic modes of expression within the traditional framework. The individual's struggle to choose and formulate a personal stance is supported, with the proviso that one first study and know the sources of the tradition, appreciate their depth and diversity, and their ability to address modern issues. The integrative option presumes that classical Judaic sources can provide important perspectives on Jewish life today, that profound and abiding human experiences inhere in the ancient texts, and that only by recovering these experiences can the relationship between the Jewish people and its literary heritage be restored (Celebrating, 1980).

In sum, the integrative option assimilates selected features of Berger's three options and creates a new approach toward the retention of tradition. It begins with Jewish tradition, with the aim of discovering its rich varieties of personal expression and the acceptance of difference. It utilizes such modern disciplines as logic, philosophy, and social science, along with the individual's immediate experience. Commitment, reason, and experience are then combined by the individual into a continuous effort at uncovering the past and integrating it with the present. One of the consequences of the integrative option is the elusiveness of attaining the final truth and completing the integration process, which leads the individual to live in a permanent state of uncertainty.

The four options can be better understood when applied to the State of Israel. The establishment of Israel has thrust religious and nonreligious Jews into the everyday world. The visions of Judaism and its dreams and mission must coexist with the mundane realities of the here and now. While some Jews who are enamored of the dream are repelled by the reality, others, rooted in the reality, deride the Jewish dream.

Those who adopt the deductive option have an image of Israel as the holy land promised to Abraham at the dawn of Jewish history and permeated with the Divine Presence. They recall the glorious days of temple worship and ceremony, and the great personages who prophesied, reigned, and studied in Israel. The modern, secular state is not sanctioned by tradition. Redemption of the Jewish people and land will come from Divine intervention and cannot be accelerated by human effort.

Supporters of the reductive option view Israel as a state among the other nations. As a nation-state, Israel has a right to create its own political, economic, and social policies under its autonomous jurisdiction. The two major features of the state are its land and its people; it is a Jewish state because Jews inhabit it. As a typical state, it is devoid of religious and spiritual endowments.

The advocates of the inductive option sense that the Jewish experience is somewhat different. When they visit Israel they feel at home and feel warmth and nostalgia, comfort and familiarity. They do not feel this way when they visit any other country. They wonder about Israel's magnetic attraction and enchantment. In order to understand their emotional experience of Israel, they begin to look to its past. It is not the state per se that attracts them, but its historical meaning and its symbolic significance for Jews throughout the centuries. They seek to connect and identify with other Jews who lived there in order to gain a more intensive historical perspective on their immediate experience.

The adherents of the integrative option insist that the great challenge of Israel is to maintain the dream and the reality of Jewish living. Israel requires the development of a mature religious attitude to life where Jews do not passively await God's unilateral intervention in history but, rather, experience God's presence in their own efforts on behalf of the total community. It is the public testing ground of the power and credibility of Jewish ideals.

> Israel shatters complacency with dreamlike Judaism; it exposes the superficiality of pulpit Judaism, culinary Judaism, and mystical Judaism. Judaism must embrace all aspects of life—the army, the farm, the city, the hospital, the nursery school, the police force. The Jew begins to appreciate the meaning of the challenge: ''In *all* your

ways know Him.'' The Israeli reality scales dreams down to a size where they can become useful and empirically meaningful; it provides the soil vital for the unfolding of a living Torah. (Israel 1981, p.3)

The integrative option poses a challenge for the modern Jew to build a Jewish society on Jewish land, to combine the essence of the dream—the past—with the legitimacy of the reality—the present, with all its incompleteness and uncertainty. Israel serves as a laboratory for the reality-testing of this approach to Jewish living in the modern world.

## CLASSICAL SOURCES OF RABBINIC AUTHORITY AND INDIVIDUAL AUTONOMY

As mentioned, the two sources of authority in Jewish tradition are Sinai, and human reason. The authority of Sinai is succinctly enunciated in the Talmud: "Moses received the Torah from Sinai and handed it over to Joshua and Joshua to the elders and the elders to the prophets and the prophets gave it over to the men of the Great Assembly (Avot 1,1)." The rabbis asked how Moses could have studied the entire Torah, since "longer than the earth is its measure and broader than the sea (Job 11:9)." Their answer was that Moses was given its principles, on the basis of which new laws that revealed the hidden meanings of the Torah were promulgated in succeeding generations.

The rabbis' response leads to the resolution of two seemingly contradictory statements: "The Torah is from heaven" and "The Torah is not in the heavens." In the former, the rabbis confirm the fundamental doctrine of the divine origin of the Law, the authority of Sinai. The latter affirms the authority of reason, i.e., man's responsibility to explicate and apply the Torah to the vicissitudes of life. Human reason, utilizing the thirteen hermeneutic principles (Torat Kohanim, Lev. 1) as analytic tools, has the ability to decipher the Torah's hidden meanings and translate its normative expectations. The future development of the normative tradition can be traced back to its origins. All insights, commentaries, and ordinances subsequent to Sinai had been, in effect, already implicit in the original Law. "The tradition of learning reflects a deep sense of human adequacy and an acknowledgement of the dignity of man. Within the Jewish tradition, the importance of learning is closely related to the model of God as the accepting, loving teacher. The student who feels the warmth and the love of his teacher is encouraged to work out the implications of what his teacher has given him. The teacher's love liberates the student to create, yet to regard his creation as an expansion of what he received (Hartman, 1978, p.26; Midrash Rabbah, Exodus 28:4)." The Jews' development of the oral tradition has the dual effect of unifying the entire religions system under the supreme authority of Sinai and granting to the individual's reason the status of co-partner in the creative process of the Word. "The Word which mediates divine love becomes integrated with the human response; the creative development of the Torah by the student and the teacher's guidance become part of one Torah. The oral Torah and the written Torah become one (p.27)."

The prophet was excluded from participating as an innovator in the legal tradition. Maimonides (1963) states unequivocally:

> And so, if a Prophet claims that God told him that the judgment—*pesak*—in any given commandment is such and that the argument of so-and-so is correct, behold that Prophet is killed; for he is a false prophet as we have explained, for there is no revelation of Torah after the first messenger (Moses) and there is no addition and no diminution, "It is not in the heavens" (Deut. 30:12). And God did not assign us to Prophets but he assigned us to wise men, masters of argument. He did not say, "And

you shall appear before the Prophet"; rather he said, "And you shall appear before the levitical priests, or the magistrate..." (Deut. 17:9). And the Sages have dealt at great length with this issue and it is correct (p.14).

Maimonides' theory of halakhic reasoning cannot permit the intrusion of appeals to prophetic authority. The theory is based on the distinction between the laws emanating directly from Sinai on which there is no disagreement, and those laws derived from the application of the thirteen hermeneutic principles where there was no Mosaic legislation. It is in this category of laws that disagreement occurs, and the decision is in favor of the majority (p.4). Disagreement does not imply disloyalty to the authority of the tradition, but is instead a legitimate response to the laws which allow for reasoned disagreement (Hartman, 1976, p.112).

The text, "It is not in the heavens" (Deut. 30:12) serves as the basis for Maimonides' theory of halakhic reasoning. Combining it with the companion text "And you shall appear before the Levitical priests or the magistrate" (Deut. 17:9), Maimonides removes the prophet from participating as a prophet in halakhic debates and judgments. "The appeal of the prophet to the authority of God is incompatible with the logic of legal deliberation. The prophet offers no room for disagreement (p.114)." Only those people who use their intellectual powers and analytical skills to frame new interpretations of pre-existing laws as the communal need emerges are fit to develop the *Halakhah,* though they argue and disagree in the process. This is the hallmark of the human input into the encounter with the divine.

What kind of personality did Judaism want to develop? What personality type would emerge from a life devoted to the Law? *The Halakhah* is a system of norms that dictates the behavior of Jews in virtually all aspects of their lives. It would be reasonable to expect that the *Halakhah* would develop the obedient personality whose primary concern is to fulfil the laws of the tradition. Yet, according to Hartman, Maimonides shows that obedience to authority is not the sole virtue of *Halakhah*. "If *Halakhah* encourages the development of a critical mind capable of independent reflection and evaluation, it cannot be exclusively characterized by appeals to authority which demand unconditional obedience (pp.104-5)." There is room for both under the sacred canopy of the law. Consequently, the *Halakhah* has fostered the obedient personality that accepts religious norms without question, and also the autonomous personality who finds the way to God and the community through the use of reason. Though the former group has outnumbered the latter throughout history, the mere possibility of the intellectual love of God—as enunciated by Maimonides—sanctions the use of argument, dispute, and disagreement that are the hallmarks of reasoning people.

The obedient personality is the type of person developed by an authoritarian system. The personality type developed by a system whose appeal is to reason is the autonomous person whose commitment is nurtured by thinking and understanding. This person can more readily appreciate the wisdom of normative Judaism and come to love God as its author, not only emotionally but also intellectually.

The two personality types reflect the two sources of authority in Jewish tradition—the authority of Sinai which claims unconditional obedience, and the authority of reason which supports individual autonomy. Autonomy implies the right to put in one's difference, to disagree, based on the cogency of argument. Both rabbinic scholars and students have the autonomy to engage in rational discourse with the law, though the rabbis' authority is more weighty, owing to their greater knowledge and piety. The student, though, is encouraged to use his or her reasoning powers to contribute interpretations to the tradition. The authority of such opinions will gain wider acceptance as the student deepens the pursuit of scholarship and tests it with others. Thus is developed the authoritative tradition of reason.

The Sages possessed more authority than the ordinary person due to the breadth of their knowledge and depth of their reasoning. Their normative interpretations of the tradition that gained wide acceptance among the populace bound the laity in their practice, though they were permitted to disagree with the Sages' supporting arguments. Intellectual pluralism has always been sanctioned in Jewish tradition, as exemplified in the case of the rebellious elder.

## THE REBELLIOUS ELDER

The case of *Zaken Mamre*—the rebellious elder—symbolizes the legitimacy of intellectual autonomy in Jewish tradition. The elder, who is a learned and wise man, disagrees with a decision handed down by the *Sanhedrin*—the Supreme Court in Jerusalem—and proceeds to practice to the contrary. His rebelliousness is punishable by death (Deut. 17:8-13).

The elder's rebellious attitude began long before the Supreme Court's decision. He had disagreed with a decision of the local court in the small town in which he lived. The majority rule did not apply because he was not one of the judges. As a scholar he was permitted to challenge the local court's judgment and to seek clarification from the higher courts.

The areas of the elder's disagreement with the court, according to Maimonides (1956, Laws of Rebels, IV), are in biblical law and rabbinic decrees, since violations of the latter eventually lead to violations of the former. Maimonides' purpose for including rabbinic ordinances is "to reduce conflict in Israel (Sanhedrin 88a)."

Maimonides considers the case of the rebellious elder as having serious implications for the continuity of social order. As the Supreme Court is responsible for establishing a unified

legal system in the nation, opposition to its decisions is a threat
to its authority and legitimacy in the eyes of the people. The
death penalty that awaits the rebellious elder is designed to preserve the honor and status of the court. To Maimonides, the
ideal Jewish community is homogeneous, functioning within a
framework of law, wherein individuals deny their practical differences with the established legal system and agree to abide by
its decrees.

In contrast to Maimonides, Nachmanides (cited in
Maimonides, 1955), limits the case of the rebellious elder to
violations of biblical law. The elder is not punished if he
violates the Supreme Court's interpretation of a rabbinic
decree. The essential difference between biblical law and
rabbinic decree is that the former is fixed and unchangeable,
while the latter varies with different times and places.

One can understand Nachmanides' position in this way.
With reference to the interpretation of biblical law, there is but
one authoritative voice—the Supreme Court—which is en-
trusted with this task. With regard to interpreting the varied
meanings of social and cultural change, there is ample room for
different perspectives. Conflict is therefore inevitable in deter-
mining the fit between old decrees and new circumstances.

Nachmanides provides wide latitude for the individual to
express his differences with the established legal authorities.
He is apparently not as concerned as Maimonides that conflict
may engender disrespect for authority. He believes that social
change lends itself to various interpretations, and the
individual, instead of being stifled, should be encouraged to
express views which may contain much insight and wisdom. In
this situation, the elder is not designated as rebellious for he
does not challenge the foundation of Judaism—the Torah—but
the court's interpretation of changing reality. The elder's use of
reason and analytical skill that may result in contrary conclusions is sanctioned.

## The Presentation before the Supreme Court

In his appearance before the Supreme Court (after having visited several lower courts who could not render a decision and who subsequently accompany him to the Supreme Court), the elder begins the procedure by presenting his argument first; the lower courts do not present their arguments. The court hears his version of both sides of the conflict. Psychologically, this procedure reduces the elder's anxiety. He is the star, as he occupies center stage. Since his is the only testimony, he can support his position with all the arguments he can muster without being contradicted by the lower courts.

Thus, despite the authoritative aura of the Supreme Court, composed of 71 justices sitting in the Temple courtyard in Jerusalem, the rabbis facilitated the individual's intellectual autonomy and encouraged its full expression before so august an audience. The right of the individual to be heard was safeguarded, and the lesser legal authorities took second place to this daring man. The lone voice was not to be stifled, for it could harbor eternal truths.

## The Arguments

There are two sources of evidence for the respective arguments: tradition and opinion. The four possibilities for differences are: both sides present their positions based on tradition, i.e., what each received from his teachers; both present opinions; the court presents a tradition and the elder an opinion, and vice versa (Sanhedrin 88a).

R. Elazar asserts that the chance for the elder to lose his case exists in all four variations—even if he claims support from the tradition and the court offers an opinion. R. Elazar is concerned with the preservation of a unified community and with the elimination of social conflict; he is prepared to sacrifice the autonomy of the individual to maintain respect for law and order.

R. Kahana claims that the case of the rebellious elder obtains only when he voices an opinion against the court's tradition. In this situation, tradition is stronger than opinion; it must be preserved at all costs, even if it requires putting the elder to death for violating it in practice. In all other situations, the elder is acquitted, and if he teaches others to practice against the court's decision, he is not culpable.

R. Kahana grants the individual a greater degree of leeway in expressing his independent way of thinking. He sanctions public expressions of difference, a form of pluralism that approves of disagreement in thought and action which does not threaten the authority of the tradition. Within that boundary, the individual may continue to function autonomously as a communal leader.

## After the Decision

If the Supreme Court's decision opposed the elder's position, he lost his case. Thereupon he could no longer teach others to practice the contrary. The entire nation must abide by the court's decision and orient its conduct accordingly (Deut. 17:12; Sanhedrin 86b). If the elder retains his position and its supportive arguments and persists in teaching it to his students, he is not culpable as long as he refrains from urging them to translate it into practice.

The mishnaic term used to designate the elder's nonculpability is *pa-tur*—free, exempt (from punishment) (Sanhedrin 86b). Does this mean that though he is exempt from punishment, he must desist from teaching, lest he inadvertently encourage defiant behavior, or is he permitted to teach, for it is certain that he will not overstep the legal constraints? Is the act of teaching his point of view seen as a positive, legitimate function, or is it a lesser evil than action?

Maimonides (Laws of Rebels III, 7) states that the Supreme Court can excommunicate, strike, and prevent the elder from teaching others. Maimonides' view is consistent with his stance regarding the preservation of social order. In the teaching process, the line between theory and practice is too fine to sanction the one and prohibit the other; the student may also misconstrue the teacher's message. In order to avoid these misunderstandings and minimize the possibility of rejecting the highest authority in the nation, Maimonides prohibits the dissemination of ideas contrary to the prevailing law.

Another view is offered that supports the elder's right to continue to teach his ideas. This is based on the Talmudic practice of listing the minority view, though the decision favors the majority. The minority was encouraged to seek biblical and logical supports for their opinion and try to outmaneuver the majority with their reasoning. Minority opinions were deemed fit to be published for all generations because there may come a time when their view will be preferred over the majority's (Eduyot I, 5). An example of an individual who refused to deny his intellectual autonomy in the face of the majority's opposition and still retained his status in the community of scholars is Akavia ben Mahalalel (Sanhedrin 88a). Though he was outvoted by the Sages, Akavia was not considered a rebellious elder because he only persisted in teaching, and refrained from encouraging action. Thus we may conclude that teaching is permitted as long as practice is not encouraged.

There is a second theme in the chapter of *zaken mamre*, the rebellious elder, in seeming contradiction to the first, that insists on strict obedience to rabbinic authority, though it is clearly in error.

> Thou shalt not depart from the word which they shall tell thee to the right nor to the left (Deut. 17:11). Even if he

> (the judge) tells you about what appears to you to be right
> that it is left, or about what appears to you to be left that it
> is right, you have to obey him; how much more is this so if
> actually he tells you about what is evidently right that it is
> right and about what is left that it is left (cf. Siphre)
> (Rashi, Deut. 17:11).

Apparently, the individual's trust in his own intuition, insight and judgment is to be denied when the judge has rendered the decision in a case. He must accept it, though his logic and experience affirm the contrary.

A claim can be made that this interpretation does not contradict the rabbis' support for intellectual pluralism, for it is addressed to uneducated individuals who do not have enough Jewish knowledge to counter the court's arguments. Their response is primarily guided by instincts and experiences. Under such circumstances, the rabbis did not permit any deviation, but required unconditional obedience. The scholarly elder, however, is in a different category. His scholarship is renowned and is evident in the cogency of his arguments. His disagreement has integrity and intellectual honesty, and can be supported by the authority of reason.

In sum, the case of *zaken mamre* is a symbol of rabbinic sanction for individual autonomy within the legal authority system. The system is not closed, demanding homogeneity in thought as in action. The rabbis felt it essential to curb acts that deviated from the religious standards lest they lead to disruption of the social order. But they went out of their way to preserve the dignity of human thought by granting it an autonomous existence, not subject to authoritarian control. As long as the elder desists from practicing and teaching others to practice contrary to the Supreme Court's decision, he is not rebellious. In our interpretation, he may persist in his doctrine and impart it to others. The rabbinic authority system obtains within circumscribed boundaries: the individual who retains intellectual honesty while preserving rabbinic authority in practice is granted the right for self-expression in public.

Uneducated individuals, however, are not granted legitimate autonomy because they have no knowledge base from which to make intelligent choices among alternatives. Pluralism is sanctioned only for the educated Jew. The educated Jew is one who studies the classical texts with the aim of penetrating the rabbinic mind and understanding Judaism's conceptions of the human experience. As there exist multiple conceptions, with an increasing knowledge and sensitivity to rabbinic exegesis, the individual begins to discern nuances of difference, some of which speak more directly than others. One discovers in the self a natural selection process, wherein one tends to identify with particular themes and viewpoints which are congruent with one's personality. That leads to a deeper identification as a Jew.

## Summary and Conclusions

Traditional authority and individual autonomy is a perennial issue in human thought and social functioning. It produces tension and strain in the relationship between teachers and students, parents and children, employers and employees, and professionals and clients. Authority derives from the status hierarchy of the social order, the possession of greater knowledge and skill, and tradition represents the continuity of values, customs, habits, and norms. The actual exercise of authority is usually based on a combination of these factors. Its realization depends on the other's willing obedience.

In the premodern world, authority was situated primarily in traditional modes of behavior, i.e., habitualized ways of living. Choices were few to nonexistent, for religion—the dominant institutionalized source of tradition and authority—preordered conduct in structured ways that left little room for questioning. Life was predictable and objectively valid, and the individual felt secure in the order provided by religious traditions.

In the modern era, perspectives are different. Due to what Weber calls the ''rationalization'' of the Western world, society has become secularized, and human functioning is more independent of persuasion based on status hierarchy. Religion has shifted from the public arena to private life. Choice is a dominant feature of social life and religion, as people choose among a variety of belief and ritual systems. Religious tradition is no longer perceived as a guide for behavior; the individual relies on his or her own insights, reason, and impulses. There is much uncertainty in the process, but also independence from authoritarian controls. The trade-off is between autonomy from ideological constraints that stifle creativity, and confusion from choosing among a multiplicity of alternatives

The most interesting outcome from this study of classical Judaic texts is Judaism's support for pluralism. The educated individual's difference with other scholars and with the legal establishment is respected and even encouraged. R. Kook's (1962) comment on the Talmudic statement, ''Scholars increase peace in the world,'' is striking:

> Many mistakenly think that world peace will only be attained when all people have the same ideas and characteristics. Therefore, when they see scholars arguing about the results of their research, they think that this is the absence of peace. In truth, this is really a mistake: true peace will come only through the development of many perspectives, differences of opinion, arguments, even matters that appear contradictory. When all the different points of view are combined, only then will the truth of the Torah appear. Therefore, rabbinic scholars actually increase peace when they contribute new and different interpretations from various perspectives, even opinions that are contrary to each other (p.330).

R. Kook's interpretation is refreshing in that it confirms a sanction which is obvious to the student of Talmud—the open expression of difference, the explication of the minority view, and the legitimation of all opinions regardless of their legal validity. This point of view was not widely accepted in Jewish communities throughout history. The dominant motif was obedience to halakhic authorities and an unquestioning, acquiescent attitude toward the normative tradition.

The discovery of pluralism enables modern Jews to take a fresh look at Judaic classical sources and tune in to their multidimensional approaches. The rabbis sanctioned multiple conceptions because they recognized the reality of intellectual diversity. Modern Jews can feel free to explore the tradition with their own analytical categories, and with an appreciation for the differences in culture and history between then and now.

The pluralistic situation has different connotations for the modern Jew who is both ideologically and behaviorally committed to Jewish tradition, and the Jew who is not yet committed in these ways but seeks to do so at a graduated pace. The committed Jew confronts pluralism on two levels: the intellectual and the behavioral. Intellectual pluralism, symbolized by the case of the rebellious elder, poses little discomfort because the *Halakhah,* Jewish Law, has openly sanctioned it. Committed Jews know that they have the support of the tradition when they offer opinions and interpretations that differ from rabbinic conceptions, for those conceptions are not uniform either. As examples, the meaning of *kashrut,* the experience of freedom at the Passover Seder, the philosophy of Shabbat, the historical significance of such biblical events as the Exodus from Egypt, the revelation at Sinai, the idolatry of the Golden Calf, the building of the Temple—these lend themselves to various interpretations and inspire creative thinking among thinking Jews. Since the tradition sanctions intellectual diversity, the committed Jew's curiosity and reasoning ability are granted full expression.

Pluralism on the level of behavior is another matter. Here, the authority of the *Sanhedrin*—the Supreme Court—was preeminent in order to maintain conformity to the law. Historically, in the absence of the *Sanhedrin*, the legal tradition, recorded in the codes and the responsa, was accepted as authoritative. Its primary function was to preserve a normative system of behavior for Jews wherever they lived. It sought to unify dispersed Jewish communities and preserve their distinctiveness among the nations.

In local communities and educational institutions such as *yeshivot*, conformity in behavior was encouraged, and deviations evoked disapproval. Although differences among halakhic authorities have always existed, local Jewish communities tended to subscribe to their particular rabbinic authority's decisions. They came to believe that theirs was the authentic way, although they knew that other opinions prevailed elsewhere. Pluralism in behavior has characterized Jewish religious life since antiquity, not only among small communities but especially between the two large traditional groupings of Jews: Ashkenazim and Sephardim. One could also point to the internecine conflicts between Hasidim and Mitnagdim that evolved into different interpretations of Jewish law and ritual. But on the individual level, subscribing to a particular rabbi's authority, and within the family, the invoking of family traditions —*minhag avoteinu b'yadeinu*—created the perception that Judaism was monolithic, that there was only one way to practice the religion.

The modern committed Jew is faced with the conflict between the perceived monolithic nature of the normative tradition and the knowledge that it is pluralistic in practice. The individual is caught between commitment to the law as stated in its codes, and the need to translate it into modern forms which may eventuate in change. The committed Jew strongly believes in practicing ancient Jewish behavior to strengthen ties to the past, but also wants to try innovative approaches to rituals to refresh personal commitment. Thus, in the process of interpretation, the committed Jew is caught between the demands of history and the attractions of modernity.

The not-yet-committed Jew does not face the intellectual/behavioral conflict of the committed Jew. For such an individual the difficulty is with the perceived obsolescent character of Jewish tradition. The impression of the Talmud is that of a legalistic document, designed to build fences around archaic biblical laws that have little meaning in the twentieth century. The ancient laws are perceived to be too restrictive, with little relevance to contemporary values and life styles. These impressions may be due to a minimal or nonexistent Jewish education, or one in which Jewish values were not applied to modern concerns in challenging ways.

The Jew who seeks affiliation and commitment will proceed slowly. Should the individual decide to perform a particular ritual, he or she may want to ascertain its purpose and meaning, may consult with friends to learn from their experiences, or experiment with different forms of the ritual, incorporating and discarding details in the process of discovery. When a particular pattern emerges, habitualization converts the earlier tentativeness into a firmer commitment. The ritual provides meaning because it is invested with meaning.

For the not-yet-committed Jew, Jewish ideology and behavior derive from the pluralistic experience. They are the result of choices from among many available options. To choose to live a Jewish way of life today, at whatever degree of intensity, requires a courageous affirmation of commitment to the Jewish people, Jewish values, and Jewish history. For such individuals and families, enthusiasm, joy, and spirituality run high, for they have embraced the tradition out of love.

Similarly, the pluralistic situation offers the committed Jew the opportunity to reaffirm a commitment out of choice and not out of habit. When one *chooses* to be committed to Jewish tradition, one's commitment is stronger and more abiding. It infuses life with more meaning and joy.

## AUTHORITY AND AUTONOMY IN PROFESSIONAL PRACTICE

One of the unique features of study at the Shalom Hartman Institute is a deep commitment to Jewish tradition, and at the same time, intellectual openness. The combination of commitment and openness seems to have been supported by the tradition itself. They are not contradictory, but complementary; they hold open the possibility of identification with abiding values, norms, and ideals, and respect for criticism, change, and difference in the pursuit of truth. How can commitment and openness be translated into a professional methodology? How can the professional's dilemma be more clearly understood?

Commitment to tradition implies loyalty to, and emotional identification with, its values, norms, and ideals, and the conviction that the tradition speaks to the individual in modern times. Commitment to the profession implies loyalty to its values, ethics, and ideals, identification with the profession as a "calling" which offers a vital service for human betterment, a means for building society.

Intellectual openness toward the tradition implies an acceptance of its nonmonolithic character, a questioning of its fundamentals, critical loyalty, and a belief that spiritual growth is achieved through maximum understanding. In the professions, intellectual openness is expressed through different conceptions of the professional role, the professional-client relationship, and the definition of the problem. There is no one way to help a person in need. A profession becomes more effective as its knowledge grows and is translated into new services. A profession becomes stronger when its committed practitioners open themselves to changing theories, roles, and services, when diversity is seen as a sign of maturity. Commitment to tradition and openness to pluralism serve as the background for a discussion of the authority-autonomy conflict in the professions. The tradition of the profession—its values, ideology, norms, and especially its knowledge base—provides the professional with important sources of authority. Pluralism in the profession inheres not only in its diverse theories and conceptions of the professional role, but in the professional-client relationship—in the interaction between professional authority and client autonomy.

In education, the methodological question that confronts the teacher is the degree to which to impart knowledge to the student, and the degree to which to enable the student to discover new insights independently. It is the perennial conflict between content and process, "material and form (Kaufman, 1961, p.714)."

The teacher's inner struggle revolves around the timing of interventions, and whether the primary function is to teach or to enable students to learn. As an example, the teacher who uses the lecture method to impart knowledge reduces the student's initiative to learn independently. Use of the seminar method reflects the belief that learning accrues through active involvement and self-motivation. There are many variables that determine teaching styles and methods, one of which is the teacher's felt need to exercise authority in the classroom, and belief in the student's capacity for autonomy in the learning process.

In various therapeutic enterprises, there appear to be different perceptions of the therapist's attitude toward patient autonomy. A student psychiatrist has claimed that "the psychiatrist undermines the patient's confidence in interpreting reality and by direct extension, his sense of autonomy. Psychiatry justifies this paternalism, in a clinical sense but one with moral overtones, by positing that the original subversion of the patient's autonomy is a means to achieving even greater autonomy at the end of therapy, when one has achieved understanding and a measure of control over the seething psychological drama of the unconscious (Levine, 1981, p.1)."

In client-centered therapy, Rogers (1976) raises significant questions regarding the therapist's respect for the patient's capacity and right to self-direction, and to what extent the therapist has a need and a desire to dominate others.

> Is the therapist willing to give the client full freedom as to the outcomes? Is he genuinely willing for the client to organize and direct his life? Is he willing for him to choose goals that are social or antisocial, moral or immoral? If not, it seems doubtful that therapy will be a profound experience for the client.
>
> Even more difficult, is he willing for the client to choose regression rather than growth or maturity? to choose neuroticism rather than mental health? to choose or reject help rather than accept it? to choose death rather than life (p.48)?

Rogers affirms his unconditional trust in the client, so that any outcome that may be chosen will be accepted by the therapist. Only then does the therapist realize the vital strength of the capacity and potentiality of the individual for constructive action. In client-centered therapy, the authority of the therapist is claimed to be nonexistent. In one client's words, "in counseling we were mostly *me* working together on my situation as I found it (p.51)."

Fundamental values of the social work profession exalt the dignity of the client and the client's right to self-determination. Social workers are deeply committed to these values but, as they begin to inquire for their meaning and their translation into practice, pluralistic interpretations arise. For example, is self-determination an absolute or a relative value? Does the client genuinely have a right to decide independently, regardless of the consequences, or is this right circumscribed by various social factors? In contrast to Rogers' client-centered ideology, Bernstein (1960) insists that self-determination is not a "king" but a "citizen" in the value hierarchy of the social work profession. It is nine-tenths illusion and only one-tenth reality (Perlman, 1965), and it is the latter that social workers need to help clients preserve.

Once self-determination is relegated to a relative value, it complicates the relationship between the professional and the client. Neither the former's authority nor the latter's autonomy can be distinctively defined, for they fluctuate with each problem and situation. There are no absolutes. There is greater openness and variability in their efforts to define the problem and their respective responsibilities for its resolution. The uncertainty could have a positive impact on the creative aspects of the helping process, but could also be debilitating for a client with a limited capacity for autonomy.

Uncertainty may also lead to more control, for the professional may believe that the client is not capable of deciding unilaterally. A review of the language social workers have used to describe their professional functions indicates a subtle shift from enhancing client self-determination i.e., autonomy, to controlling it (Keith-Lucas, 1963). Following Rogers, there is a real question regarding social workers' trust of clients' ability to take responsibility for their own lives. In their struggle to maintain a balance in the authority-autonomy dichotomy, social workers quite naturally sometimes incline toward one over the other. But as they reflect upon their actions, their skills, experience, and insight enable them to try to correct the imbalance the next time.

It is apparent that there are many variations in the professional-client relationship with regard to the authority-autonomy dichotomy. Each profession needs to clarify its approaches to deal with the inevitable tensions that arise in the relationship between professional authority and client autonomy.

This chapter has endeavored to make a formidable claim for the individual—the "significant other" in the authority hierarchy. Now attention turns to the family to examine this issue in the relationship between parents and children.

*Chapter 2*

# AUTHORITY AND INDEPENDENCE IN JEWISH FAMILY RELATIONSHIPS

The modern Jewish family finds itself at the crossroads of the waning influence of tradition and the increasing incursion of modernity. The decline of authority is a consequence of the former, and the pluralization of choices is a feature of the latter. It therefore becomes more difficult for parents to impart a particular value system to their children when other systems are available. The proliferation of multiple value orientations is a function of the sociocultural setting which poses serious value conflicts for the modern Jewish family.

Three modern trends in social life appear to threaten the traditional values that have undergirded Jewish family life. Their impact is subtle and gradual but nonetheless real and disturbing. These trends are: technological obsolescence, quantified time orientation, and narcissism.

It is futile to attempt to turn back the march of technological progress. However, it is important to be aware of its impact on our consciousness and behavior. Technology exalts the new and deprecates the old. Obsolescence is its inevitable by-product as it searches for ways to create new material needs to satisfy people's thirst for novelty. What is old is useless not only in terms of machines and gadgets, but also people. Hence the devaluation of the aged in modern society and their relegation to second-class citizenry.

Authority, too, becomes obsolescent, and increasingly subject to challenge by children and adults due to the rapid rate of deinstitutionalization (Berger and Luckmann, 1967, p.81) and the negation of traditional values in an era of social and cultural change. It is expected that children will rebel against their parents and workers against their employers. The generational cleavage seems to be unbridgeable.

People's time-orientation is futuristic; there is discontinuity with the past (Berger, 1977). Events do not flow from the past to the present, for time is spatialized and quantified—a constant series of new beginnings. Modern people believe they can control time, and deny the wondrous possibilities inherent in the experience of time as a continuum from the distant past to the endless future, and the opportunity to help shape the future from the perspective of the past.

This memory-less time sense is an outgrowth of the value orientation induced by technological civilization, and it too exerts a profound impact on consciousness and behavior. Those whose birth antedated the individual at least by a generation, i.e., parents and certainly grandparents, are perceived as belonging to the past. Their values are felt to be old-fashioned, outdated, and no longer relevant to a fast-moving, future-oriented society. Disrespect for persons in authority as a function of age differentiation is a widespread phenomenon.

A third modern trend, closely allied to the others, is the appearance of the "new narcissism" (Lasch, 1978), a "trend toward the deification of the isolated self" (Marin cited in Reiner, 1979). In contrast to the normal narcissism of the young child, this narcissism seems to be a more profound and deviant form of individualism, for it arises from feelings of irrelevance and loneliness. The individual is out of touch with others and prefers to go it alone. He or she perceives no real value in community, and is primarily preoccupied with the self.

Individualism and narcissism are processes that threaten family continuity. Not only do they undermine the values of family and community which foster togetherness, giving of self, and belonging through the social context of the group, but they promote the antithetical values of singlehood and marriage without children. Some may rationalize their option for single-hood and a childless marriage by expressing their concern over the possibility of a nuclear disaster and ecological imbalance due to overpopulation. In fact, they really seek personal pleasure and self-realization—goals with which a spouse and children usually interfere due to their own need satisfactions. Families require mutual concern and a caring attitude. When one marries and has children, one adds uncertainty and risk to one's life because the future of these relationships cannot be foreseen. Children growing up in the culture of the "new narcissism" learn that taking is more pleasurable than giving, and being served is more rewarding than serving. Even the group is perceived as a means for self-gratification. Relationships are primarily functional and self-serving. Family life in this cultural context can degenerate into serious conflicts between parents and children whose values and needs clash with each other.

The Jewish family in modern society has internalized these cultural values into its life style. It is, therefore, deeply upsetting to observe its growing instability as reflected in rising rates of singlehood, divorce, intermarriage and declining fertility rates and of drug addiction, delinquency, and alcoholism.

This chapter is an effort to counter this trend ideologically through a penetrating study of some of the traditional Jewish sources—biblical, Talmudic, and rabbinic—regarding the relationship between parents and children, which will bring to the present a fresh perspective on family relationships. The focus is on the authority of parents and the independence of chil-dren—their distinctive values, the tensions emerging from their interaction, and their interdependence.

Upon entering the world of Jewish tradition, it becomes apparent that value and behavioral structures have been established to guide and regulate parent-child relationships. The first impression of this particular world is that of the massive weight of authority, attested to by the *mitzvot,* the *Halakhah,* and the *responsa,* *—comprising the extensive legal system that institutionally coerces behavior and consciousness. So, too, is the parent-child system conceived as one in which obedience to parental authority is the sacred norm permeating family life.

A deeper penetration into the family structure reveals a perspective that serves as a check on parental authority. Judaism perceives children as having needs of their own for growth and development and thus, to be granted various measures of independence from parental authority. The *Halakhah's* sensitivity to children's need for independence counterbalances the requirement of unvarying obedience to their parents' authority. Both thrusts obtain in the relationship and both are sanctioned by the law. An analysis of these familial patterns will afford a deeper understanding of how Judaism views the interaction between parents and children, their mutual obligations, and the inevitable tensions that arise in this relational system.

This chapter is divided into five parts:

1. Parents as symbols
2. Parents as real people
3. Honor and fear: differential patterns of relationship
4. Authority and independence
5. Parental obligations to children

The *Mitzvot* are the biblical precepts which traditionally number 613. The *Halakhah* encompasses the entire system of Jewish law; the *responsa* comprise the question-and-answer literature that emerged in Jewish communities after the Second Commonwealth. The recorded legal decisions were incorporated into the *Halakhah.*

## PARENTS AS SYMBOLS

In much of the traditional literature that includes the Talmud and biblical commentaries both ancient and modern, there is a significant emphasis on parents as symbols. They are seen as symbolizing major values and ideals in the Jewish community. Children's obligations to obey their parents not only obtains on account of their direct ministrations to them, but because of what they represent. Parents serve as a medium through which children enter the Jewish world of faith, ideals, history, and community leadership.

### God

God as the central motif in Jewish life occupies the central position in the parental authority structure. All biblical commentaries explain the location of the commandment, "Honor thy Father and thy Mother...(Ex. 20:12)" among the first five of the Ten Commandments as signifying the identification of respect for parents with respect for God. The Talmud also equates them on other levels.

> The Rabbis taught: it says, "Honor thy father and thy mother" and it also says, "Honor the Lord with thy substance" (Prov. 3:8)—the Torah equated the honor of father and mother with that of God; it says,"You shall fear every man his mother and his father"(Lev. 19:2) and it is written,"Thou shalt fear the Lord thy God and serve him"(Deut. 6:13)—the Torah equated the fear of father and mother with the fear of God...(Kiddushin 30b).

The Talmud discusses this relationship not only in symbolic but also in experiential terms. It attempts to esteem child obedience beyond the meaning that it has for parents.

The Rabbis taught: A person has three partners: God, his
father and his mother. When a person honors his father
and his mother, says the Holy One, blessed be He, it is as
if I am dwelling among them and they are honoring me
(Kiddushin 30b).

Respect for parents is ideally designed to serve as the relationship model of respect for God. God is the child's father,
once removed, even as He is the father of the Jewish people.
"You are children of the Lord your God.(Deut. 14:1)." God's
presence in the family constellation and His critical observa-
tions regarding the child's behavior toward the parents could
awe the child and place responsibility upon him for unqualified
obedience. God-consciousness enforces the authority-obedi-
ence system and constitutes the core of family cohesion. When
there was community support, such as in the East European
*shtetl,* children accepted instruction and discipline even though
they did not understand the reasons. The authority of the
parents was backed by the ways of the group and the commandments of God (Zborowski & Herzog, 1967, pp. 335-6).

In the relative absence of transcendent authority symbols
today which could provide a framework for the relationship
among family members, parental authority is weakened, and
the family becomes exclusively an instrument for personal
growth and development. It lacks cohesion because each member's vision of the future is self-oriented.

## Tradition and History

Parents not only represent God to their children, but Jewish tradition and history as well. Samson Raphael Hirsch
expressed this idea in his commentary on the fifth
commandment.

The knowledge and acknowledgment of historical facts
depend solely on tradition, and tradition depends solely
on the faithful transmission by parents to children, and on

the willing acceptance by children from the hands of their parents. The continuance of God's whole great institution of Judaism rests entirely on the theoretical and practical obedience of children to parents, and *kibbud av v'em* is the basic condition for the eternal existence of the Jewish nation (Hirsch, Exodus 20:12).

Parents are the means for bringing God into the life of the family and perpetuating Jewish tradition by teaching it to their children. The authority of parents is a prerequisite for ensuring the authority of the tradition; obedience to the former will enable the child to accept the latter. Concomitantly, the authority of parents is reinforced by the authority of the tradition. Thus, as each reinforces the other, the child is exposed to a massive authority system that encompasses the entire Jewish past and is realized in the present.

In another approach to the historical representations of parental authority, Hartman explicates two of the Talmudic obligations devolving upon parents. The father is bound to circumcise his son—*berit milah**—and to redeem him—*pidyon haben*.** The Jewish boy must be introduced into the covenant of Abraham, the founder of the Jewish people. The task of parents is to demonstrate that a Jew is the progeny not only of biological parents but also of a man whose identity was based upon a complete transformation of values. One of these is to dare to stand up to the culture of the time and proclaim one's difference—a difference based upon ideals, beliefs, and values. Another is to represent this ideology by living it, despite the

*The *berit milah* is the act of circumcision of the male child which Abraham as the first Jew performed. It represents the covenant between the Jewish people and God and is a symbol of Jewish identity.

**The *pidyon ha-ben* is the ritual performed with the first-born male child 30 days after his birth. It represents the child's redemption from the tenth plague in Egypt during which the first-born of the Egyptians died. It is, therefore, symbolic of the redemption from slavery and the Exodus.

opposition of the majority. "The *berit* is a symbol of Jewish identity; a person is not defined by genetic constitution alone, but by norms and ideals (Hartman, 1978, p.79)."

The duty of *pidyon ha-ben* obligates the parents to introduce the child to the memory of Egypt. Father and mother must transmit a knowledge of reality outside of the child's experience. They must "provide frames of reference rooted in the memories and the history of the covenantal community of Israel (Hartman p.81)." This history, of which the Exodus was a turning point, tells the child not to become enslaved to any human being, nor even to an idea, and that Jews must develop their own culture, ideals, and philosophy in their own land.

Hartman views parents not only in terms of their *obligations* to create a sense of memory and historical consciousness in their child, but as the *link* that ties the child to the story of the past. The notion of "link" could be extended from what they *ought to do* to what they *are*. Parents themselves symbolically represent history, for their origins appear to be in the distant past in the time-consciousness of the child. Thus Jewish parents represent Jewish history even as they are duty-bound to transmit it to their children (Ralbag on Exodus 20:12). They represent this history in their person, and when they perform rituals with historical significance, the child sees the history come alive through their actions.

These two parental symbols—God and Jewish tradition and history—can serve to restructure the time-consciousness of the modern Jewish family. In a society where time is quantified, the past negated and obsolete and the future glorified, Jewish parents represent the antithesis of this time-awareness. They communicate to the child the memory of events gone by that have shaped the Jew's values and world outlook, and the history that is continuously being re-enacted that lends sanctity to the flow of eternal time even in the here-and-now.

## Authority Figures

Parents represent not only God and Jewish tradition and history to their children, but also other authority figures. The Talmud states that "Honor thy father" includes one's older brother (Ketubot 103b) and this is extended to others who are as "fathers" to their students, namely scholars, the prophets, the aged, and the great Sanhedrin (Abarbanel on Exodus 20:12), i.e., to adults who hold high status in the Jewish community and whose authority commands respect.

Hirsch extends the significance of parental authority beyond its symbolic representations to the psychological development of the child himself.

> The overruling of the will of the parents over its own will, the cheerful yielding of its own will to that of the parents is the first, earliest, and most lasting school of practicing self-control, which leads young human beings out of the life of enforced obedience to one's urges, into mastery over one's passions and impulses, into freeing the godly element in man into that moral freedom, the achievement of which constitutes the character of *kadosh* (Hirsch on Leviticus 19:3).

The development of self-control—the *sine qua non* for the religious and social life—is attained through the child's obedience to parents. The child thereby learns how to develop a relationship to God and to other authority figures. In Judaism, obedience to parents facilitates the acceptance of the yoke of the commandments, learning the Torah from teachers, and respecting the aged and the scholars, thus contributing to a stable social order and the continuity of tradition. Through control of the impulses and development of the superego, the child is freed to enhance individual capacities and potential. By internalizing notions of right and wrong in personal actions and in interpersonal relationships, the child has incorporated the rudiments of independent functioning in society.

## PARENTS AS REAL PEOPLE

The reasons that have been advanced to explain the Torah's commandment for filial respect tend to fall within the rubric of what Blidstein calls, "the ethos of gratitude" (1975, pp.8-19). The *Sefer Ha-Hinnukh* draws the portrait of this motif succinctly:

> A man should realize that his mother and father are the cause of his being in the world, and therefore it is truly proper that he render them all the honor and do them all the service he can. For they brought him into this world, and they labored greatly on his behalf during his childhood. (Mitzuah 33)

Others cite parents' moral instruction rather than birth as a motive for filial piety, "for in bringing him into this world, their own pleasure was their motive (Blidstein, p.17)." Children, then, owe their parents respect because they gave them life and struggled to provide for them and teach them moral values.

Here, too, the tradition poses a higher value to be achieved through filial obedience. It was expected that the child would be grateful for the "good done him by the Lord, Who is the cause of his being...it was He who brought him into the world... (Sefer Ha-Hinnukh)" The child would learn gratitude to God through expressing gratitude to parents in concrete forms of service.

The obligation to honor is defined by the Talmud as providing parents with food, drink, clothing, and helping them to enter and leave their house (Kiddushin 31b). It is readily apparent that the young child and adolescent are not called upon to provide these services for their parents; they, in fact, receive their parents' care during their formative years. It would be more appropriate to apply the *mitzvah* to young adults and adults whose parents are becoming older and require personal care.

> The whole aim of this commandment is to secure positive support for aging parents from their children, who are themselves assumed to be mature adults. When families lived together in large groups, aging parents who could no longer work were entirely dependent upon their children to support them economically. It is this care of the old that is demanded here (Clements, 1972, p.125).

Care for aged parents is equated with care and honor for the old (Abarbanel on Exodus *20:12*). The provision of concrete services is a sign of respect, of *kavod*. In a similar way, Maimonides (1956) interprets the commandment to love one's neighbor as oneself as requiring such concrete demonstrations of affection as visiting the sick, attending a funeral, and rejoicing with the bride and groom (Laws of Mourning, XIV).

The reward of respecting parents is great: "that thy days may be lengthened on the earth which the Lord thy God gives thee (Ex. 20:12)." Abarbanel (1956) applies the principle of "measure for measure" to explicate this verse, i.e., those who respect their parents will have children who will respect them in their old age. Their reward will be twofold: the achievement of old age and respect from their children. "Therefore," concludes Abarbanel, "the *mitzvah* is designed not only for the benefit of aged parents but for the benefit of the child who honors them (Ex. 20:12)."

Parents are to educate their children to relate to others, including themselves, as real people with human needs, and not only as symbols. In the family, children learn how to develop emotional relationships with others, they learn how to give of themselves and deeply care for another's welfare. They learn that dependency is not an infantile state but a necessary condition to develop mature social functioning in adult life.

By obligating parents to represent the authority of the past and the adult world of the present, and the child to relate to parents as real people by satisfying their basic human needs, Judaism aims to foster a close emotional relationship between them. It sees the family as the crucible in which the child develops the capacity to be human.

In sum, Jewish tradition has invested parents with authority that claims a variety of representations, and with responsibilities that transcend those of providing material sustenance for their children. The tradition perceived in the microcosm of the parent-child relationship the possibilities of teaching children to believe in God, to internalize moral values and religious law, to identify with the Jewish people's history and drama, to respect elders in various social contexts, and to develop self-control mechanisms that are the hallmarks of adult behavior in society. The institution of the family was viewed as the conduit for the continuity of the people, their values, aspirations, and eschatological visions. Parents were given the burden and the opportunity.

The tradition believed that parents had the capacity and the potential to fulfil these expectations. It was quite aware that some parents will fall short and others won't succeed at all. The reality, by definition, would never achieve the ideal, but the ideal needed to be enunciated nevertheless. Childrearing was therefore a burden for parents, but also an opportunity to shape Jewish destiny.

## HONOR AND FEAR: DIFFERENTIAL PATTERNS OF RELATIONSHIP

The commandments to honor parents (Ex. 20:12) and revere them (Lev. 19:3) are interpreted by the Talmud in behavioristic terms. Honor, or *kibbud,* requires positive acts of service such as feeding, washing, dressing, etc. Reverence or *yirah* requires refraining from behavior that might cause embarrassment, such as sitting in one's father's place, speaking before one's turn, and contradicting (Kiddushin 31b). Fathers and mothers are to be treated with deference naturally shown a superior.

Both honor and reverence are expressions of inner personal valuation; they are not merely behavioristic roles, though they take those forms. The deed is a means of maintaining the relationship between parent and child. Certain *mitzvot* are related to acts; others are indicative of relationships. In its definition of *kibbud* and *yirah*, Judaism gives examples of the concrete acts which outwardly reflect the child's feelings for the parents.

If they are performed perfunctorily, there is a gap between the act and the stated goal, and the relationship is tarnished. *Kibbud* and *yirah* reflect the emotional bonds that a child has with the parents.

An example of the quality of the relationship expressed through service to parents is recorded in the Babylonian and Jerusalem Talmuds (Kiddushin 31a, b; 20b).

> Abimi, son of R. Abbahu recited: One may give his father pheasants as food, yet this drives him from the world; whereas another may make him grind in a mill and this brings him to the world to come.

The Jerusalem Talmud amplifies this.

> A man once fed his father on pheasants (which were very expensive). On his father's asking him how he could afford them, he answered, 'What business is it of yours, old man, grind (i.e., chew) and eat!' On another occasion it happened that a man was engaged in grinding in a mill, when his father was summoned for royal service. Said his son to him, 'Do you grind for me, and I will go in your stead, the royal service being very hard.'

A closer examination of *kibbud* and *yirah* reveals dichotomous demands upon the child.

> The *mitzvah* of *yirah,* which arouses in us the association of subjugation and obedience to external authority, pits the child against the world that preceded him. In this world, represented by his parents, there exists a system of values which the child did not select, and which he is compelled to fulfil as if imposed. This world demands his awareness and confirmation through obedience and loyalty.
>
> The *mitzvah* of *kibbud,* by contrast, which arouses in us the association of honor and valuation that flow from identification, brings the child into a world of closeness and love for his parents' values, a world of gratitude towards parents who exerted themselves in his growth and development. In this framework the child brings to expression his inner feelings, that is, his independent personality (Marx, 1980, p.1).

Acts which express *yirah* require emotional distance and self-restraint; acts which express *kibbud* require emotional closeness and action. *Yirah* is equated with parental authority and child obedience whereas *kibbud* is an expression of the child's own initiative to express love for the parents. Theoretically they are distinct, but practically they can coexist, as when the child is ministering to the parents and confronts a situation where the temptation is to correct the father's mistake. Just as Soloveitchik describes the dynamics of the Adam I-Adam II relationship as a constant oscillation from one realm of existence to the other (1965, pp.3-65), so too can the child's relationship with the parents be characterized as moving toward and away, as self-expression and self-restraint, emotional closeness and respectful distance.

If the father wishes, he can set aside-*mekhila*-his authority, thereby relieving the child of certain restrictions on behavior

(Kiddushin 27a). He is instructed not to impose demanding *kibbud* requirements on his grown son, nor strike him when he disobeys, lest the son rebel and thereby fracture the relationship (Yoreh Deah 240, 19). Apparently, because the rabbis were more interested in developing a family relationship of closeness and love, they permitted the father to drop some of the trappings of his authority when the situation called for it. They realized that it was easier for a parent to demand obedience than to foster love, and so they encouraged the latter at the expense of the former.

In sum, it has been shown that Judaism makes paradoxical demands of approach and withdrawal on the child in the relationship with the parents. While these behaviors can be seen as complementary, they can also be felt as contradictory in certain situations. This relationship model bears resemblance to other relationships such as that of friends, husband and wife, and teacher and student, where both parties relate on the level of function, i.e., distance, and on the level of feeling, i.e., closeness. The child thus learns the fundamentals of human relationships in the context of the family.

The emotional consequences of acts of *kibbud* and *yirah* can help the child to overcome narcissism. These acts require that the young person move out of the subjective world into the world of the parents. The child must recognize them as real people and not just as ideas and projections. This is particularly true for the adult child who can be so busy with career and family as to relegate parents to the past days of childhood, so that they exist now only as ideas and symbols. Jewish tradition says that one must move out of one's own world—the world of economic striving, creative endeavors, and social status where so many of one's relationships are functional and utilitarian—and become involved with one's aging parents on a deeper level than heretofore. The satisfaction of parents' needs precedes one's own. *Kibbud* and *yirah* are imaginative prescriptions for overcoming narcissism in adulthood.

In some cases, however, parents may abuse the *kibbud* and *yirah* requirements by making inordinate demands which tax their children's filial devotion and breed resentment. Nevertheless, the tradition, recognizing that not all parents are perfect, still proclaims the benefits that can accrue from a healthy parent-child relationship.

## AUTHORITY AND INDEPENDENCE

Having reviewed the expectations placed upon children in their concrete behavior and emotional responses, we proceed to explore the possible tensions that may arise when parents exercise authority, and children seek independence. Several questions guide our discussion: Are there any limits to parental authority? When does parental authority end and child independence begin? Are there any situations in which the normative tradition sanctions child disobedience? What is the relationship between authority and independence in the Jewish family?

Weber's (1947) definition of authority as "the probability that a command with a specific content will be obeyed by a given group of persons (p.152)," is useful for our purposes. In contrast to power, authority implies willing obedience on the part of followers. This definition seems to be more appropriate for designating the parent-child relationship in Judaism than that of Friedrich (1972) who defined authority as "reasoned elaboration", i.e., the ability to explain and give reasons for one's commands (pp. 45-56). In Jewish history parental authority was apparently not based on rational elements. This is borne out by the example of family life in the East European *shtetl*. "Any explanation of parental edict that is offered is apt to be in terms of sanction rather than of reason (Zborowski and Herzog, 1967, p. 336)."

Independence implies a process that leads to self-reliance, the possibility of developing one's skills and abilities through self-motivated thought and action. It is a commonplace that parents want their children to be independent human beings and to fashion a life of their own. Children strive to achieve the same goal. However, the definitions of the goal may differ, as well as the processes that lead to it. In every family there occur the inevitable clashes between the authority needs of the parents and the independence struggles of the children. This "will struggle" usually characterizes the preadolescent and adolescent stages, but it frequently occurs in young adulthood and in later stages as well.

Our analysis of the Judaic attitudes toward this developmental issue encompasses two aspects of the authority-independence continuum: limitations on parental authority, and parental obligations to children.

### Limitations on Parental Authority

There is a type of situation of which the Sabbath is an example, where parental authority is circumscribed by an external source, namely the Torah, without the stimulus of the child's aspirations for independence. This limitation is due to a difference in values and not to the child's developmental needs.

### 1. The Sabbath

The Torah states: "Every man shall fear his mother and father and observe my Sabbaths, I am the Lord (Lev. 19:3)." The juxtaposition of *yirah* and Sabbath observance encouraged the Sages to insist that children may disobey parents when told to violate the Sabbath, for "you and your parents are obligated to honor me (Rashi on Leviticus 19:3)." Honoring God is a higher law and a more exalted value than the honor of parents.

The case of the Sabbath illustrates restrictions in matters pertaining to God-person relationships. The first stage, then, in the process of limiting parental authority and moving toward child independence is based on the legal authority of the *mitzvot* to which parents, too, are subject.

## 2. Interpersonal Relations

The *mitzvot* of interpersonal relationships afford a wider arena for children's self-expression and greater sanction for their independent strivings. "If a father commanded his son not to talk with someone and not to forgive him until a specific date, and the son wants to restore the friendship immediately if it weren't for his father's edict, he need not heed his edict (Yoreh Deah 240, 16)." The commentaries based this law on the higher value of the *mitzvah* not to hate another Jew; thus the father is, in effect, commanding the son to violate the Torah (Shach and Taz, Yoreh Deah 240, 16).

The child's personal needs seem to be reflected in this situation which deals with the importance of friendship. The son wants to be reunited with his friend and his father wants to prevent it. Regardless of the father's reasons, the law comes down on the side of the son and trusts his judgment. Here, the son takes the initiative to reach out to his friend. The same decision holds true for a daughter. The case illustrates movement along the authority-independence continuum where the child's self-assertion in interpersonal relations, in effect, succeeds in curbing the parents' authority.

## 3. Intellectual and Moral Development

The child's movement toward independence continues in the realm of intellectual and moral development—the study of Torah. "If a student desires to study Torah in another city where he is confident he will succeed in his studies due to the particular teacher there, and his father protests because he fears the physical threat of the non-Jews in the city, the son need not listen to his father in this situation (Yoreh Deah 240, 25)."

The father's concern is a real one—the safety of his son. And yet, the son's need takes precedence, for he has discovered a teacher who will inspire him to study and develop his intellectual acumen. How could this yearning for learning and growth be stifled? The law, therefore, encouraged the child to pursue his interests. The stated reason is that "the study of Torah is a greater value than the honor of father and mother (Yoreh Deah 240, 13)." for it is incumbent upon both child and parents. This appears to be another concession to children's needs for intellectual and moral development, and thus, increasing independence from parental authority.

Historically, during the formative years of Hasidism there were cases similar to the one above. Children left home against their parents' wishes to study "at the table" of the Hasidic *rebbe*-rabbi. Their parents, who tended to be *mitnagdim*—opponents of Hasidism—viewed the *rebbes* as rivals for the minds and hearts of their children, and mistrusted their motives. Many children subsequently left their homes permanently and became disciples of the *rebbes*. Parents mourned for their "lost" children, and the relationships were thus broken.

Inevitably the question was asked of the *rebbes* as to whether such actions were permitted under the law, since obedience to parental wishes was a paramount value in Judaism. Invariably the answer was a resounding "yes" with various sources invoked to support the decision (Uryan, 1976). Although the environment of the *rebbe* was sometimes more authoritative than the home, nevertheless it was the child's decision to determine where to go. As such, this historical example corroborates the law's siding with the child to disobey the parents in the pursuit of Torah study.

A story is told of the son who went to study with the *rebbe* of Kotzk against his father's wishes. Upon his return home, his father asked, "What did you learn at the *rebbe's* table?" The son answered: "The Torah begins with 'In the beginning God created the heavens and the earth;' God created the beginning—the rest is up to man to complete (p. 228)." The story contained an obvious message for the father. Parents give life and sustenance to their child, but there comes a point in development when the child must take the initiative and rely upon personal resources. And this is as it should be, for Judaism sought to encourage individual initiative even where there appeared to be Divine intervention opposing the decision. In the famous Talmudic dispute between R. Eliezer and R. Yehoshua, when the *bat kol*—voice from heaven—sided with R. Eliezer, R. Yehoshua exclaimed, "We do not heed the voice of God to decide disputes." When God was asked for His reaction to R. Yehoshua's declaration, He replied, smilingly, "My children have defeated me, for they have applied my law—the law of the majority—and I cannot overrule them (Baba Metzia 59b)." This story teaches us that human initiative can transcend divine intervention.

There are two parallels to this story. The teacher provides the student with the rudiments of knowledge that enable the building of a new edifice of intellectual constructions, and parents provide the fundamental skills of being human, thus enabling the child to function in society as an independent person.

## 4. Marriage

In former times, selecting a marriage partner was usually the prerogative of the parents. Whether it was done through the *shadchan*—marriage broker or privately, the prospective bride and groom usually had little influence on the decision. This pattern was in sharp contrast to the dating and courtship patterns in the modern age, where the dominant element is free choice in the selection of marriage partners. These contrasting styles of mate-selection serve as the backdrop for the following case:

"If the father protests the son's decision to marry a particular woman whom he (the son) has chosen, the son need not heed the father (Rama, Yoreh Deah 240, 25)." The son has apparently resisted the cultural trend and selected his own bride. The law is prepared to accept and trust the son's decision, though his father may have persuasive arguments to the contrary. The same decision applies to the daughter.

Two reasons are offered by the commentaries. The father cannot deter the son's obligation to marry, because under Torah law it is considered a *mitzvah*, "When a man has taken a wife...(Deut. 24:1)." Clearly, the law is invoked by these commentaries to override parental authority. The other reason is that the son's selection of a marital partner is not under the rubric of parental authority (Baiur Hagra, Yoreh Deah). Only those matters which pertain to the physical needs of the parents (concrete acts of *kibbud*) and to their integrity and dignity (*yirah* acts of self-restraint) are subsumed under their authority and compel obedience from the child.

Marriage, which pertains to the child's private life, personal happiness, sexual fulfillment, and creation of a family, is a decision that ideally should emanate from an independent person who is engaged in fashioning a future, though parents, too, have a stake in their child's marriage. This principle is boldly stated in the Torah: "Therefore shall a man leave his father and his mother and cleave to his wife, and they shall be one flesh (Gen. 2:24)." This verse affirms the necessity for maintaining boundaries between parents and children. It is addressed to the married couple and implicitly to their parents. Parents must let go and children must separate from them in order to establish a new family of procreation. The process of independence does not begin with marriage, but for all practical purposes, it is consummated at that stage in life.

In sum, the child's movement from dependence to independence was observed to be a gradual process that affected different levels of functioning. In the child's relationship with

God, the Torah severely restricts parental authority when the direct violation of a *mitzvah,* such as the Sabbath, is involved. In the child's interpersonal life, freedom is granted to oppose the parent's restrictions on social relationships. In intellectual and spiritual strivings, the child is permitted to attend the school of personal choice. In selecting a mate, the child may oppose the parents' wishes, being deemed mature enough to decide this matter. It is here that the commentaries invoke the principle of separate domains of authority and independence.

The four illustrations seem to reflect the developmental process of the child. Sabbath observance is usually taught during early childhood, friendships take on greater prominence at the onset of adolescence, intellectual and spiritual development is a phenomenon that assumes significance during adolescence, and marriage is the task and goal of the young adult. With entry into marriage, the child has left the parents' home and has begun an independent life.

## PARENTAL OBLIGATIONS TO CHILDREN

It will be seen that independence is not only a function of the child's need to grow up and become a separate person, but also a function of the parents' responsibilities to the child.

The Talmud imposes six obligations on a father: ''The father is bound in respect to his son, to circumcise (him), redeem (him, if he is firstborn), teach him Torah, take a wife for him, and teach him a craft. Some say to teach him to swim too (Kiddushin 29a).'' The mother is exempt from these particular obligations.

The duties of *berit milah*—circumcision—and *pidyon haben*—redemption of the firstborn—require the parent to introduce the child to the covenant entered into between Abraham and God, and to the Jew's historical memory as symbolized by the Exodus from Egypt (Hartman, 1978, pp. 80-81). Both acts, occurring during infancy, imprint upon the child the indelible essence of Jewish identity in its physical and spiritual dimensions. As the child becomes an adult, confirmation of this identity is expected through the performance of concrete actions that reinforce the belonging to an historical community. Both *berit milah* and *pidyon haben* represent the religious rituals that parents are obligated to transmit to, and practice with, their children. Religious rituals are distinctively Jewish acts which possess rich historical meanings. They create a Jewish ambience in the home and serve to strengthen and deepen identities.

The father is expected to teach his son Torah, as knowlege of God's law is essential for spiritual growth. In addition to imparting knowledge, he creates a living environment which embodies educational values. "Values are not only transmitted through formal learning but also through the living and intimate community of the family (Hartman, p. 84)." Parents are expected to teach by example, a more impressive and enduring form of moral education.

Jewish tradition has decreed that the father serve as the teacher to his children, even though it permits the transfer of this role to the more formal educational network. The mother's primary role is to provide the children with physical and emotional sustenance. Each establishes a qualitatively different relationship with the child.

> The differential functions reflect a fundamental incongruity between both parents and the child. Father disengages himself from his son, while mother moves toward him via emotional attachment. The disengagement is occasioned by the father's expectation of the child's independence in learning. The mother's attachment is organically based. She can never forget that her son was part of her and that she gave him her blood (Linzer, 1972, p. 93).

In the traditional world, the parents' differential relationships with the child were commensurate with the existing social expectations. Roles of father and mother were distinctive; the father was usually the educator and the mother the housewife-nurturer. These roles were confirmed by the community and thereby strengthened and perpetuated. Under such circumstances, it is understandable that mothers would tend to have deeper emotional ties with their children than fathers who focused on discipline and intellectual development.

In the modern era, these relationships have undergone significant change. Roles are no longer fixed; there is overlap and more sharing between mother and father, particularly if both are gainfully employed. Mothers may be out of the house for longer periods than fathers. Fathers who assume domestic role-sharing may be more emotionally involved with their children than mothers. On the other hand, fathers today tend not to fulfil the educational role in the family, and instead leave it to surrogates. The family portrait that existed in traditional times appears to be more complex in the modern era; it is therefore difficult to make generalizations today regarding the differential relationship patterns between parents and children.

In the traditional family, the father's task of teaching his son Torah accelerates the son's increasing independence. Torah learning ideally develops critical thinking, analytical skill, moral growth, and meaning and guidance for everyday living. It fosters a sense of responsibility ''to the normative dreams of the community of Israel (Hartman, p. 86)'' and to the child's quest for self-realization.

The liberating aspect of the father's Torah teaching is the child's capacity to disagree with him in matters of Jewish law. Fathers enable children to surpass them by providing them with intellectual tools that foster independent thinking and the capacity to challenge the authority of ideas. Some negative consequences of this parental function include the academic underachievement of some children who are induced with guilt due to their inability to surpass their parents' accomplishments or live up to their expectations. Such children are often rejected

by their fathers because they have failed to live up to the traditional ideals of the paternal role (Linzer, pp. 92-108).

Today the obligation to teach Torah to one's son applies
equally to one's daughter, in order to ward off threats of assimilation. By Torah is meant a comprehensive Jewish education
that extends beyond *bar* or *bat mitzvah* age. Such Jewish education may not guarantee strict adherence to *mitzvot,* but it can
foster a deep sense of Jewish identity. Jewish identity today
requires constant reaffirmation, particularly through study and
the performance of distinctively Jewish acts, in unison with
other Jews.

Parental responsibility for the marriage of their children in
the modern era does not entail the selection of mates, but an
expression of concern for their physical and emotional needs.
Parents need to create a home environment which fosters the
psychological capacity to love. This entails the ability to
assume responsibility for oneself and for others. Children need
to experience love and responsibility within their family in
order to transfer these capacities to their own spouses and families. Parental authority, then, needs to be tempered during the
adolescent's transition into young adulthood to enable the
development of self-confidence and life goals.

Parents also have to make it possible for the child to feel
liberated from a sense of guilt for abandoning them. The popular stereotype of the Jewish mother holding on to her child
tenaciously through psychological pressure and "guilt trips"
should no longer hold true among second and third generation
American Jewish families. Parents need to let go and encourage their children to make it on their own. Real independence
is achieved in marriage, and Jewish tradition requires parents
to facilitate this process.

The obligation to teach one's child a trade is aimed at providing the young person with a source of economic dignity to
avert overwhelming financial stress and dependency. Economic independence is perhaps the most critical index of self-

reliance in adulthood, and a major component of a secure self-image. Parents who exert a significant effort in this regard are making an important statement regarding their aspirations for their children's productive contributions to society. A child who needs parents' economic support tends to feel very dependent and less of a man or woman. Parents can be said to have failed in this regard when their children have no means of financial support in their young adulthood.

At times the society also contributes to the state of dependency. In Israel, young married couples cannot afford to purchase apartments for themselves because of their prohibitive costs, and rentals are not the norm. They are compelled to ask their parents for help and/or devise alternative ways to raise the funds. In Israel, and increasingly in America, having a trade would still not suffice in enabling the individual to purchase a place to live. In the kibbutzim, however, dwelling places and material needs are provided in exchange for labor and commitment to the ideals of sharing in the kibbutz's future.

The Talmud does not expect the father to set up his son for life; it rather expects him to provide the rudiments, the initiative, the curiosity about the world that would motivate the child to learn, to explore, and to translate those beginnings into a form of work that is emotionally satisfying, socially productive, and self-sustaining.

In requiring the father to teach the child to swim, in order to save himself from drowning when the boat capsizes, the Talmud apparently insists that the child must learn how to deal with unpredictable crisis situations in a competent manner. Teaching the young person to swim may also be viewed as analogous to teaching him or her how to drive a car and how to defend oneself. Apparently the obligation is to help the child to develop competence in order to function in society, to acquire the skills to maintain a job, handle an interview, act responsibly, and deal with stress and crisis. Swimming symbolizes the everyday acts a person is called upon to perform that attest to competence and maturity.

It is apparent, then, that the entire thrust of the parents' obligations to their children is to help them to grow up and become persons in their own right. Their charge is to assist them to gain independence through the developmental process. Yet, even as they strive for self-realization they are bound to the restrictions of the family's authority structure. It is this interplay that will now be addressed.

## Summary and Conclusions

The writing of this chapter has brought me to the discovery that authority and independence are not two distinct phenomena in Jewish family life, but are in full interaction and interpenetration. Early in the research I sensed that an inordinate emphasis was placed by the biblical commentaries on *kibbud* and *yirah* that denoted parental authority and filial responsibility. There were few references to limitations and none to independence. Thus my dominant perception of the Judaic value hierarchy was that it inclined more toward parental authority than to child independence.

A clarified picture emerged from my encounter with the Talmud and the Code of Jewish Law. The parental obligations to children listed in the Talmud point to the direct relationship between the functions of the parent and the independence of the child. The primary function of the parent through the teaching role is to make possible the child's growth. It is akin to the teacher's role with the student where dependency is discouraged in order to enable the student to develop a capacity to think and reason. In the family situation, parental function is obligatory irrespective of the child's demands. Parents, upon becoming parents, obligate themselves to care for, raise and prepare their child for the real world. In the memorable words of an elderly woman during a discussion, "If you bring children into the world, you have to take care of them."

Another source of the child's independence was discovered not in the parental function but in the psychological development of conscience. Hirsch, in explicating the concept of *yirah,* suggests that reverence and respect for parents enable the child to learn self-control and mastery over passions and impulses, thereby leading to the achievement of moral freedom (Hirsch, Exodus 20:12). Freud calls this process the development of the superego, which is a prerequisite for mature social functioning. By internalizing parental authority, the child psychologically becomes the parent, and becomes free to function independently. The child knows the difference between right and wrong, whereby personal behavior is guided by a system of values. The capacity to become independent is acquired while being dependent; it emerges and coexists with the experience of interdependence.

Our entry into the world of Jewish tradition began with first and second impressions. The first impression was that of a weighty system of authority layers that Judaism placed upon the shoulders of parents to transmit and represent to their children. The second impression took note of Judaism's respect for the child's need to be independent. Initially, the authority layers seemed more awesome and important than the drive for independence. Now the parent-child system is perceived to be in exquisite balance. Neither can demand total obeisance. There is ample time and opportunity for authority and independence to coexist harmoniously during the child's growth process. Judaism has established a ''check and balance'' system to insure that parents will be served and their dignity preserved by children whom they will help to grow up to become independent persons. Parents and children need each other to grow from their interaction as a family unit and as individuals.

I began with a discussion of the negative impact of certain sociocultural value orientations on the moden Jewish family. The value conflict can now be posed. In a society where obsolescence is a built-in dynamic in the materialistic lifestyle, and time is an element to be controlled and quantified, parents and certainly grandparents appear as anachronisms. The best years of their lives—their youth—are perceived to be a thing of the past, and their future is limited. They are out of date and old-fashioned.

I conclude with an appreciation of contrasting values that Judaism has invested in family relationships. Jewish tradition esteems age, history, the spirit. An old person is not out of fashion, but one to be honored. History is not outdated but omnipresent in the consciousness and behavior of the family. The life of the spirit is esteemed, for it reflects God's presence in a family where mutual respect, love, and transcendent values characterize family relationships.

The family that attempts to lead a life based on these Jewish values can succeed in combating excessive individualism and narcissism. There is a healthy balance between parental needs representing the group, and children's needs representing the individual. The cohesive family not only unites its individual members but encourages them to identify with the family *qua* group. Thus the family becomes a transcendent entity where the individual contributes to its ongoing even while encouraged to foster his or her own development.

*Chapter 3*

# MODELS OF AUTHORITY-INDEPENDENCE RELATIONSHIPS IN THE MODERN JEWISH FAMILY

The presentation of the authority-independence model in the previous chapter did not discuss its application to the modern Jewish family. My intention was to explore Jewish traditional attitudes toward the mutual obligations of parents and children, and to let the findings and interpretations stand by themselves.

After presenting this model to a group of adults affiliated with the Shalom Hartman Institute, I realized that this gap must be bridged. The group discussed the model from their vantage point as professionals and as parents. They raised many questions concerning its viability in modern times and even in premodern times.

This chapter is a response to their questions. It discusses the applicability of the authority-independence model in different historical periods, its testing in a short-term counseling situation, and the problem of authority in the modern Jewish family. Three variations of the model are then presented that reflect three types of modern Jewish families.

## THE AUTHORITY-INDEPENDENCE MODEL IN HISTORY

One of the problems inherent in the authority-independence model is that it has not been prominent in Jewish history. It is difficult to find a Jewish family whose style of living consciously balances parental authority with child independence. Apparently, in the traditional Jewish community, independence is not a value of which there is keen awareness. It is an assumed quality of the nurturing process which is part of the taken-for-granted character of everyday family life.

Authority is the central concern because only through the force of authority can important values be transmitted to children. The Jewish legal system sought to create a framework for normative family living wherein filial obedience to parents regardless of their age is unquestioned. Such training in respect and reverence could easily be transferred to other significant adults. Thus, the continuity of the tradition would be ensured by imbuing in children respect for, and obedience to authority, rather than through the development of their independence.

The rabbis of the Talmud presented several examples of the tests to which children were subject in order to affirm their obedience to their parents and to refrain from criticizing their actions.

> R. Tarfon had a mother for whom, whenever she wished to mount into bed, he would bend down to let her ascend; (and when she wished to descend, she stepped down upon him). He went and boasted thereof in the school. Said they to him, ''You have not reached half the honour (due); has she then thrown a purse before you into the sea without your shaming her? (Kiddushin 31b)''

The text does not specify whether R. Tarfon's mother demanded this form of obedience from him or he offered it voluntarily. Regardless, it is to be noted that the rabbis compared their acts of *kibbud av va'em*—honoring father and mother—with each other to see whose were more extreme and consequently more laudatory. Another rabbi offered an even more extreme reaction to the obligation of honoring parents.

R. Johanan said: Happy is he who has not seen them. R. Johanan's father died when his mother conceived him, and his mother died when she bore him (Kiddushin 31b).

R. Johanan was happy because he was relieved of the *mitzvah*; he felt that he could not fulfil it adequately. But perhaps his statement is a rationalization for not having parents to love and respect.

When the rabbis wanted to illustrate additional models of filial respect, they cited instances from non-Jewish families.

It was propounded by R. 'Ulla: How far does the honor of parents (extend)? He replied, Go forth and see what a certain heathen, Dama, son of Nethinah by name, did in Askelon. The Sages once desired merchandise from him, in which there was 600,000 (gold denarii) profit, but the key was lying under his father, and so he did not trouble him (to wake him to take the key) (Kiddushin 31a).

Another incident involving the same person is even more pronounced.

When R. Dimi came, he said: He (Dama, son of Nethinah) was once wearing a gold embroidered silken cloak and sitting among Roman nobles, when his mother came, tore it off him, struck him on the head, and spat in his face. Yet he did not shame her (Kiddushin 31a).

During the Talmudic period rabbis were apparently more concerned with filial obedience than independence, which they discussed infrequently. This may be due to their fear of the possible consequence of independence: rebellion against Torah values and way of life.

In other periods of Jewish history, the parent-child relationship did not focus on obedience but on the perpetuation of the tradition. There are many examples of fathers who expect their sons to carry on the tradition, for the future of *Am Yisrael*—the people of Israel—depends upon their commitment. Witness Isaac and Jacob's pledges to fulfil Abraham's destiny to be the father of the Jewish people, Aaron's children to perpetuate the priesthood, Solomon's reign as the continuation of David's dynasty. During and after the Middle Ages, there were many instances of fathers who left ethical wills, in which they sought to commit their children to enact the Torah's teachings in their lives and perpetuate the parents' moral teachings. Ethical wills point out the way to the children, and are a practical, behavioral-guide type of literature. For example, Elijah, the Gaon of Vilna, advised his sons not to set foot outside their houses unless it was absolutely necessary, in order to avoid interrupting their study of Torah. He even advocated praying at home because they could be distracted from Torah study by the many people congregating in the synagogue (Encyclopedia Judaica, 16, p.531).

The ethical-will literature points to the major priority of Jewish families in the course of Jewish history: the preservation and transmission of the tradition. To achieve this goal fathers saw fit to function as the authoritarian head of the family in raising and educating their children. They were strict in demanding discipline and conformity to religious and ethical standards of behavior. The child had to obey teachers and elders too, for they were an extension of the parental authority system.

The fostering of the child's independence, i.e., the right to decision-making and nonconforming actions, did not assume priority in parental tasks and was not even a value. Perhaps parents were afraid that independence might lead children away from normative Jewish living, or they assumed that the natural growth process would lead them toward independence. One is hard-pressed to locate examples of parents who encourage their children to decide their life style for themselves in such matters as education, vocation, and marriage. The major community standard for successful parental functioning was the children's conformity to Jewish values, morals, and teachings. Thus parental authority could claim a social control function rather than a liberating function in the self-development of children.

In the East European *shtetl*, a paradigm of a traditional Jewish community, it was unimportant for children to understand the reasons for a particular instruction and for disciplinary action. "You were told that you mustn't do certain things, but you were never told the reason why. But we understood that it just wasn't right. And we obeyed," is a typical statement of a person who had grown up as a child in the *shtetl*. Obedience to parents was "blind;" their authority was unquestioned. In intellectual matters, however, notably the study of Torah, questioning and challenge were encouraged and approved (Zborowski and Herzog, 1967, p.336). It was through the vigor of argument that independent and rational thinking was developed in young people. Through deciphering its intricate meanings, the student makes the Torah his own, and thereby effects a transfer of ownership from God to man (Tosafot, Sanhedrin 19a). The *shtetl* offers a good illustration of the priorities of parental function. Parents did not view their primary goal as the development of their children's independence; it was an assumed fact of child-rearing (Zborowski and Herzog, p.331). By not inviting questioning regarding rules and regulations, they thereby sought to maintain an atmosphere of unquestioned authority. But in the study of Torah, a paternal responsibility, the seeds were sown for the future direction, spiritual leadership, and ongoing of the Jewish community.

In sum, this discussion has shown that the authority-independence model had not materialized with any degree of prominence in Jewish history. Instead, the preservation of parental authority was a greater value than the fostering of children's independence.

## TESTING THE MODEL IN A SHORT-TERM COUNSELING SITUATION

I had an opportunity to test the authority-independence model during a lecture tour of the north of Israel, in the city of Safed. In one of the community centers, I was asked to give a presentation to parents of Sephardic origin on parent-child relationships in Jewish tradition. Due to a variety of snags, only one man attended. The problem that he presented was simply stated. S. and his wife have three sons, aged twenty-one, sixteen, and twelve. The family is traditional: they observe the Sabbath, *kashruth*, and daily prayer service accompanied by the *tefillin*—phylacteries. The younger sons abide by the cultural norms of the family; they pray daily and the sixteen year-old dons *tefillin*. S.'s problem is with his twenty-one year-old, who is in the army and does not pray daily. S. feels deeply hurt and ashamed that one of his children no longer maintains the tradition. He argues with him frequently and berates him. He asked me for an approach that would persuade the son to change his ways. S. had not succeeded by being authoritarian. He was pleased, though, by his son's respectful demeanor in not violating the sanctity of the Sabbath when he comes home for a visit.

In my assessment of the family situation, I sensed that my objective would differ from that of S. I knew that I could not prescribe a formula for S. to persuade his son to return to the tradition; but I felt I could help him understand the underlying issues more clearly. I defined the problem as a conflict between the self-image and pride of the father who labors hard and long to maintain his family's ties to each other and to Jewish tradition, and the son's assertion of his need to be independent of parental control. It evoked the classic tension between authority and independence, set in a cultural context: the immigrants' determination to preserve their traditional values versus the second generation's desire to acculturate and discard the yoke of the tradition.

I decided to approach the problem by sharing Judaic insights into parental authority and child independence, since this was the original purpose of my visit. Because I expected the outcome to be the opposite of what S. had anticipated, I was prepared to give him a great deal of support for his efforts as a father, and to suggest the direction in which he should move in relation to his son.

I indicated that the *Halakhah* accepts a duality in parent-child relationships: the expectation that the child will respect the parents' authority, and the latter's limitations, as when the child opts to be assertive, such as in the cases pertaining to friendship, Torah study, and marriage (Yoreh Deah, 240). In addition, not only must the father recognize the child's needs and wishes, but the *Halakhah* also required him to make possible his son's growth into an independent person (Kiddushin 29a).

Having shared this information with S. I was prepared to support his efforts on behalf of his family. I acknowledged his claim of hard work to support his wife and children, how he has taught the boys and provided them with a good Jewish education, and maintained a traditional home with a respectful, loving atmosphere. His authority in the home is still unquestioned, for when the son returns, he conforms to the family's norms in religious observance. The other children are following in S's footsteps. But the elder son has now asserted his difference from his father. Though it difficult for S. to face this challenge, it was a reality with which he must contend.

I felt that I should present the legal limits to parental authority in order to join the issue for S. and situate it within his religious framework. Parental authority is confined to the particular issues that directly address the parent-child relationship; those issues pertaining to the child's private life are beyond the control of the parent. The parent must let go, painful though it may be. Letting go, however, does not preclude his involvement and influence in the decision-making process, although the decision and its consequences must be the child's.

Here, then, was an approach for S. to consider in working through the relationship with his son. I pointed out to S. that at age twenty-one the young man had a right to live his own life, even as he continued to be a faithful son in the family. I cautioned S. to restrain himself from berating his son for his behavior, and cited the law that a father may not strike his grown son lest he turn from him (Yoreh Deah 240, 20). I interpreted "striking" not only in a physical sense but also verbally. I encouraged S. to continue to influence his son's values and conduct, which were his prerogatives as a father.

I did not deal with the culturally based tensions between father and son for several reasons. At the time, I did not locate the conflict in that context. It was only later, upon reflection and discussion with others, that the cultural element in the generational conflict emerged as significant. In addition, my primary focus and mental set was on my educational function in the lecture I had prepared, in which Jewish classical sources were applied to the parent-child relationship.

The session lasted 45 minutes. I do not know whether I helped S. to resolve his problem, but I think he gained some clarity on some of the issues. He seemed gratified by interview.

## Authority in the Modern Jewish Family

The discussion thus far has reviewed the historical viability of the authority-independence model and found it wanting because, as the primary source for preserving the continuity of the tradition, parental authority was stressed over child independence. The case example was a brief effort at translating the model into a contemporary family conflict situation. It serves as a bridge to a discussion of authority in the modern Jewish family.

In the traditional Jewish family, parents had grown up within a milieu that was supported by the culture of the community and the history of the people. Presumably they had already internalized the various authority figures in the Jewish community—parents, rabbis, teachers, and elders. They could comfortably represent these figures to their children and teach them to respect and revere them.

The burden was placed upon the child to believe in God, to accept His authority and that of his or her elders without question, and to abide by the laws and customs which governed family and community life. To the modern consciousness, this burden seems to have been awesome, for in inspiring fear and reverence, it seemed also to signify a negation of the child's own will. To be taught and reminded that God is present in the home could conceivably condition the child to develop self-consciousness and guilt feelings whenever he or she disobeys a parental order or acts in an undisciplined manner.

The tightness of the authority system might seem claustrophobic to the modern mind but it was not so perceived by those growing up within that milieu. The outside observer tends to exaggerate the restrictions of a heavily institutionalized system of behavior, but the insiders perceive it as a taken-for-granted way of life. Those who grow up within the system tend not to feel repressed. In fact, the institutionalization of their lives eliminates much decision making and leaves room for innovation. (Berger and Luckmann, 1967, pp.72-79). The problem arises when children opt to leave the system because they deem it oppressive. This creates a schism between the generations that threatens the continuity of the system. This phenomenon usually occurs with an immigrant group and their second-generation children, as for example, in the United States around the turn of the twentieth century, and in Israel with the immigration of diverse Sephardic communities in the 1950s.

In the modern Jewish family, by contrast, the burden of sustaining the values inherent in parental symbolism—God, Jewish history and tradition—rests primarily with the parents. They need to actualize these symbols on an ongoing basis in order for them to have real meaning in their everyday lives. Otherwise as parents they represent mainly themselves, and the task of asserting their authority in that role becomes more problematic. Modern parents' role as authority figures is exhausted by whatever weight of authority they can muster from the adult world of the here and now, for it is not buttressed by the authoritative tradition of the past.

The reasons for the disconnectedness from the past are obvious to the discerning eye. Belief in God and faith in His ministrations are anathema to the modern, secular consciousness. They play a minimal role in child-rearing which is heavily influenced by the scientism of modern psychology. Similarly, ritual practices, when they do obtain in the home, are mediated to the child infrequently, without their intrinsic meaning, and often with the intention of countering the rituals of the Christian majority (Sklare and Greenblum, 1968). They tend to be perfunctory, superficial and present-oriented; they lack the depth and the historical meaning that were meant to be conveyed by their performance.

When the parental symbolic system is weakened because its external supports, i.e., religion, tradition, and history are lacking, parental authority must be drawn from the nuclear family itself. Father and mother should ideally command respect and obedience because of who they are—older, wiser, more mature, and as providers for their children. Their authority emanates from themselves when they act with firmness and consistency, setting appropriate limits and establishing boundaries, making decisions and abiding by them, teaching both formally and informally, and imparting values explicitly and by example. Parents should be leaders.

This task is eminently more difficult in a society where age, wisdom, and maturity are not esteemed over youth, self-reliance, and egalitarianism. These latter values, buttressed by the value of individualism, undermine the effectiveness of authority. They challenge the taken-for-granted character of the authority of elders. Under these circumstances, parents are thrust back upon their own selves to devise ways of coping with the challenge to their authority, and with the need to confirm their identity as parents. Stable identities are hard to come by for they require stable plausibility structures which do not exist (Berger, 1979). Parents in nuclear families appear to be quite alone in their efforts to assert their authority and to gain the acquiescence of their children.

The problem of authority in the family is a microcosm of the problem of authority in larger social institutions. Though they comprise such elements as objectivity, historicity, and moral authority, institutions are perceived to be mainly coercive. They force the individual to act in prescribed ways. In a stable society, where stable institutions comprise the social order, parental authority is taken for granted because it is supported by the larger institutional framework. The coercive element in the parental role is internalized by the child, so that obedience is not externally imposed but willingly granted.

In a society of rapid change, new values, mores, and life styles constantly appear. There is an emphasis on experiencing the present and the felt need to be an individual, to do things one's own way without the need to conform to historically predetermined patterns. When the individual begins to question why one must behave in the institutionally prescribed way, this initiates a process of deinstitutionalization. The individual has more leeway in weighing alternatives and making decisions; thus one is thrust back upon one's own skills and perspicacity. Some are equipped to handle this opportunity for independent thinking while others become easily confused because there is a paucity of external guidelines and internal controls. There follows considerable experimentation with different forms of the institutional behavior. Various patterns of behavior emerge which often lead to confusion and uncertainty.

There are important social consequences of the process of deinstitutionalization. ''The ability to act with committed concern, compassion, and caring for each other is diminished when institutions lose the shape of their definition and the force of their function (Setleis, 1979, p.148).'' Other important elements of social experience are also lost, such as purpose, prescribed behavior, reciprocity of roles, expectations, values, and sanctions. It is as if the anchors for locating the individual in society were loosened, leaving one to fend for oneself in the stormy sea of conflicting options.

Parental authority is intimately bound up with the stability of the institutional order. When the latter is weakened, so is the former. When the society is faced with institutional breakdown, the restoration of parental authority becomes a yeoman task, particularly in the Jewish community. In its traditional stereotypical forms, with the stern, disciplinarian, emotionally distant father and the doting and loving mother at the family's helm, this family type is anathema to the highly acculturated, middle-class, educated Jewish family of today. Not only can this portrait not be restored, but it could not be very effective in child-rearing practices.

The egalitarianism that currently characterizes marital relationships also affects the relationship between parents and children. The distance that an authoritarian presence fosters is no longer a viable option. Instead, new forms of relationships based on democratic principles have been emerging. The structural changes that ensue affect both traditional and assimilated Jewish families.

To delineate these issues more fully, three models of Jewish family life will be presented, as variations of the authority-independence ideal-type model: the authoritarian model, the egalitarian model, and the mediating model. Each of these models is represented by a particular segment of the Jewish community: the Hasidic family, the assimilated family, and the traditional family.

## THE AUTHORITARIAN MODEL

The authoritarian model is a variation of the authority-independence model in that it stresses the central, organizing role of parental authority in the family, and does not concern itself with actively promoting child independence. It is a carry-over from previous eras, and in fact seeks to perpetuate the form of family life that predated modern times. "The patriarchal family is authoritarian and autocratic with power vested in the head of the family, and with the subordination of his wife, sons, and their wives and children, and his unmarried daughters to his authority (Burgess, Locke, & Thomas, 1963)." This family model could be found throughout Jewish history and most recently, in the East European *shtetl*.

The group in the modern era that portrays this model of family orientation is the Hasidim. Notwithstanding variations among their sects, Hasidim seek to preserve *shtetl* culture amidst secular society by residing in circumscribed geographical enclaves, maintaining distinct forms of dress and language, and a social structure where the *rebbe*—rabbi—occupies the most prominent position in the community (Poll, 1979).

The rabbi-disciple relationship in the Hasidic community has symbolic significance for the parent-child relationship. The disciple views the *rebbe* as a *tzaddik*—pious, holy person—to whose authority he submits in most areas of religious and social life. The social process governing their relationship parallels Weber's description of the charismatic figure's relationship with his followers (1947). For the believers the *rebbe's* word is law and must be obeyed. There is no room for questioning his authority and no initiative to decide for oneself. Disciples ask such questions as whether to initiate a particular business venture, to marry a particular person, and how to resolve interpersonal problems, in addition to the typical requests for his prayers in time of illness and misfortune in their families.

In the family, the father views himself as the unquestioned authority figure, to whom his wife and children show deference. His is the major responsibility for educating his children to be learned and pious Jews, and for creating an atmosphere in the home wherein the tradition would be transmitted through intense Jewish living. He demands excellence from his children in Torah study, and does not permit secular culture to be brought into the home.

The strengths of this model are numerous. It strives to ensure the continuity of Jewish tradition through the fusion of the father's authority as parent and as symbol of the tradition. It succeeds in raising obedient children who will easily transfer this trait to their relationship with other authority figures. It provides for a clear demarcation of the domestic roles of father and mother, thereby reducing confusion among family members regarding self-identity and the norms of interpersonal relationships.

There are also disadvantages. Despite its efforts at self-isolation, the Hasidic family is exposed to the cultural mores of the larger society. One of these is the adolescent's freedom of mobility and independence. Another is the woman's rights to self-fulfilment as a person, and not just as a housewife and mother. This ideology supports the wife's liberation from total subservience to her husband and household duties, and her entry into the world of education, work, social and cultural affairs and ideas. The wife's growing dissatisfaction with her traditional role creates conflict with her husband, as she demands more of his involvement in the nitty-gritty chores of family life and freedom to pursue her personal interests.

The societal trend of questioning authority threatens the father's tendency toward authoritarianism. Interpersonal ties in the Hasidic family tend to be less cohesive in an open, changing society. The father's efforts to transplant an authoritarian model of family living which originated in an earlier epoch are bound to encounter frustration, conflict, and at times, failure. Perhaps the rising rates of divorce, drug dependency, and delinquency in the Hasidic family can be partially attributed to the father's determination to perpetuate an anachronistic family life style that leaves little or no room for compromise. The psychological impact on children also needs to be taken into account. Children tend to develop a punitive superego which results in obsessive-compulsive behavior. This could be due to several factors, including the father's excessive demands on the children's educational performance and ritual conformity, and the children's inability to oppose both the father's and the tradition's authoritarianism. They want so much to please their parents by granting them the *nachas*—joy—that they so eagerly await, but they sometimes fall short of their expectations.

While there are considerable benefits accruing from this model of family relationships, its disadvantages make one hesitate to recommend it as a viable option for the majority of Jews. Most Jewish families could not envision themselves leading an existence that is self-insulated, authoritarian, and a cultural carry-over from premodern times. They prefer to be part of the larger society and deal with the stresses resulting from the acculturation process.

## THE EGALITARIAN MODEL

In contrast to the authoritarian model, the egalitarian model emphasizes equality among family members and parental responsibility to develop children's independence (Burgess et al, 1963). It is attuned to the child-orientation in Western

societies in which children's needs and predilections are in-
dulged. Where possible, children are given their own rooms in
the house. This has the effect of fostering privacy and individuality within the family, and independence in children
(Seeley, Sim and Loosley, 1956). Parents tend to downplay
their authority and the emotional distance that it evokes;
instead they seek to develop closer ties with their children by
emphasizing their common interests and goals.

The ideology supporting this model is based on the egalitarian principle. This principle suggests that roles should not
be demarcated along vertical lines, but along horizontal lines.
Sharing follows interaction, and both are necessary for decision
making. One of the innovative forms of the decision-making
process is the family council meeting in which all members
express their ideas and feelings on family matters and each
other's conduct, and arrive at decisions via democratic principles. Everyone, including parents, is liable for criticism—a
family norm that does not imply disrespect but is designed to
assure conformity to the family's moral standards. Everyone
has an equal vote on issues, so that parents cannot invoke their
authority arbitrarily whenever it suits their needs. The effect of
this structural pattern is to enhance children's independence
and their greater equality with parents and thus practically eli-
minate the hierarchical structure of the family's authority
system.

The egalitarian model, at the opposite pole from the authoritarian model, has been adopted by the modern assimilated
Jewish family, which is heavily influenced by the ideology of
feminism. The wife works and perhaps has a career. She may
be a professional in her field of endeavor, having attained
advanced degrees. She views herself as in the process of self-
actualization. The husband is either a businessman or a professional. eagerly pursuing personal advancement and lucrative
success. The family's socioeconomic standing is upper middle-
class.

As a Jewish family, its inclination is to assimilate into the larger society with, at best, tenuous ties to the Jewish community. The diminution of the authority system is accompanied by the absence of distinctive Jewish behaviors and firm commitment to Jewish continuity. Pluralization is the norm. The family feels comfortable rearranging its social structure because it is not significantly influenced by traditional forms of Jewish family life. It sees itself primarily as living in the present, and is not burdened with the weight of historical models. As choices abound, it feels it can innovate in many different ways, discard those that prove ineffective, and incorporate those that work.

Families subscribing to the egalitarian model need to work hard at maintaining the desired equilibrium among their members. For parents who had been raised in authoritarian-type homes, this task is even more difficult. The tendency to transfer one's childhood model into adulthood is tempting, and easier than creating a new model of relationships within the family. Yet, if the commitment, the ideology, and the patience exist, such families can be successful in maintaining mutual respect and fostering the more rapid independence of children. However, with the absence of ties to the organized Jewish community, the children would inevitably be lost through assimilation and intermarriage. As such, this model does not bode well for Jewish survival.

## THE MEDIATING MODEL

The mediating model takes, as its starting point, the definition of mediating structures offered by Berger (1977). "Mediating structures are those institutions which stand between the individual in his private sphere and the large institutions of the public sphere (p.132)." The large institutions breed alienation, for they are often remote, impersonal, and unsatisfactory as sources for individual meaning and identity. By contrast, private life, which is experienced as the single most important area for the discovery and actualization of meaning and identity, is underinstitutionalized. Its lack of structure, in effect, asks the individual to create his or her own private world *de novo*, with few and unreliable institutional supports. Private life is always under the shadow of anomie. A mediating structure such as the family attempts to reduce alienation and anomie by supplying the individual with social supports that contribute to his or her location in society and provide meaning and identity.

In the mediating model, the family does not mediate between the private and public spheres of the individual, although it functions in that capacity too. Rather, it mediates or fosters interaction (Schwartz, 1976) between tradition and modernity, between the memories of the religious past and the experience of the secular present, between the role clarity of Jewish families in pre-modern times and their role ambiguity in the modern era. The mediating family struggles to apply the richness of the past to the experiences of the present in order to anticipate the uncertainties of the future.

The Jewish family that perceives itself to be a mediator tends to be traditional in its orientation. Its outlook on the world is colored by Jewish traditional values and its conduct is regulated by ritual practices. It is neither exclusively Orthodox, Conservative, or Reform, but a family type whose primary identity is permeated by Jewish consciousness and behavior. It struggles to mediate between the conceptual and behavioral demands of Jewish tradition and the ideologies and conflicting life styles of modern society. The mediation process is difficult because it requires the translation of Jewish values and concepts into a modern idiom, in order to cope with antithetical Western cultural values. The family experiences this difficulty not only intellectually, but also experientially, because it wants to partake of the secular culture in depth. Its marginality induces a continuous dialogue with the conflicting forces of tradition and modernity, and unending efforts at their resolution.

The straddling, or, as Berger puts it, the "pluralization" of these two worlds affects the relationship between parents and children. There is a fusion between authoritarianism and democracy, between controls and limit setting by parents and the participation of children in family decisions. The requirements of *kibbud*—honor—and *yirah*—reverence—are not strictly enforced; the father's insistence on preserving his honor is compromised by his *mekhila*—renunciation—of this demand. Parental authority is introduced more softly and children's independence is accentuated more seriously than in the typical institutional family. The family strives to maintain a balance between the emotional needs of the parents and the developmental needs of the children.

Fathers and mothers are torn between the time demands of the world of work and those of their family. The conflict is joined for each within his/her own role configuration. The father feels responsible for the economic well-being, moral standards, educational achievements, and Jewish life style of the family, having internalized this role from paternal models in his family and in Jewish history. In order to carry out these functions, he needs to spend time with the children, and time is a scarce commodity in the bustle of modern living. It is, therefore, the *quality* of his interactions with his children into which he invests his efforts.

The mother's conflict is similar to that of the father but with some variations. If she is working, the time pressures are greater because she ultimately feels responsible for her job and her household. Her exposure to feminist ideology challenges her to justify and value identification with the traditional role of mother. As a mother she is committed to educate informally and to instill Jewish values in her children, an objective she could not achieve if all her efforts were spent on actualizing herself. She perceives herself to be a vital link in the chain of the *masorah*—tradition—and firmly believes that her priority is to raise Jewish children who will contribute to society and to the perpetuation of the Jewish community. She is, therefore, willing to put self-development in second place.

Another component of the mother's prioritization of family over self stems from her identification with the maternal role exemplified by *her* mother. She wants to maintain the *aishet hayil*—woman of valor—image, though in different garb. She translates traditional ways of raising children and caring for the home into modern forms that retain loyalty to the internalized image of her mother, but take account of more numerous options.

This type of family insulates itself enough from the larger society in order to preserve a Jewish traditional way of life within its confines, but it is open enough to permit many of society's cultural patterns to enter. The family receives support for its efforts by associating with similar families in Jewish organizational networks. These plausibility structures and the activities which they offer reinforce the identity of the family as one that is traditional and modern at the same time, and enable it to share conflicts and frustrations with other families who are undergoing a similar ideological struggle.

## Summary and Conclusions

The thrust of this chapter has been on the paucity of legitimations from Jewish history regarding the viability of the authority-independence model in real life. It was, therefore, categorized as an ideal type, from which were developed three alternate models of parent-child relationships which are more attuned to the diversity of Jewish family life styles in modern times.

These models may be similarly designated as ideal types, for it would be difficult to find their representation in Jewish families in pure form. The authoritarian family permits some egalitarian forms of decision making. The egalitarian family may not be totally assimilated, and may, through its affiliation with the Jewish community, introduce mediating forms into its Jewish experiences. The mediating family may be egalitarian in some respects and authoritarian in others. The individual explication of each model helped to clarify its distinctive properties and provided the opportunity for delineating the variety of Jewish family types more accurately.

While the independence of children is inherent in the family's functions and sanctioned by the tradition, the traditional Jewish family did not stress it as a primary concern of child-rearing. Instead, efforts were invested in insuring the continuity of the tradition through religious instruction, ritual behavior, and moral examples. Thus was created the obedient personality in diverse authority systems. Children's independence was not an issue.

It is, however, an issue today, and families struggle to find different ways of coping with it. The three models illustrate some ways in which Jewish families deal with the tensions of parental authority and child independence. The authoritarian family tries to follow its historical antecedents in perpetuating traditional Jewish life by denying individual initiative that might lead to deviation from halakhic norms. The Hasidic family is the modern prototype of the authoritarian model.

The egalitarian family, by contrast, deemphasizes parental authority and encourages children's independent initiatives. It introduces democratic procedures into family interaction. What holds the family together is the members' mutual respect and interdependence gained through valuing individual differences, and their openness to new experiences both within and without the family. Relationships are open and free-flowing, not closed and controlled. The pluralization of choices in values, religion, and life styles affords this family greater freedom regarding its participation in organized Jewish life.

The mediating family stands between the past and the present, between tradition and modernity. It derives values and memories from the tradition that sustain its determination to live in a changing society. Since it needs to learn how to deal with potentially corrupting influences on its value system and behavior code such as current sex mores, political and business corruption, and the self-actualizing orientation, its adherence to Jewish tradition helps it to confront such value conflicts directly. With the tradition's support, the mediating family situates contemporary ethical and moral trends in their cultural context, and distinguishes them from Judaic approaches. Its priority is on the family and not on the self. Obligation and duty take precedence over personal rights.

In reality the mediating family does not always succeed in negotiating the inherent tensions in its predicament. Parents and children are in conflict regarding the satisfaction of their own needs vis-a-vis family obligations. The equilibrium between the two opposing forces is not always maintained. Value conflicts are not always mediated successfully. It is an ultimate goal toward which the family strives, although the proximate steps to attain it are not always clear. This family lives with uncertainty in its attempts to juxtapose two worlds.

The mediating model stands between the extremes of the authoritarian and egalitarian models. The authoritarian model is too insulated for the modern consciousness, and the egalitarian model is too unstructured, and uncommitted to the preservation of the Jewish community. The mediating model is proposed for adoption because it has the best potential for Jewish survival in modern times. Because it occupies the middle ground, this model can help parents and professionals discern variations in the family's life style and consider alternative options to strengthen Jewish commitment even as it pursues the attractions of modern culture.

The task of modern Jewish families, even of individual Jews, is to mediate the contact between the Jewish past and the secular present. They need to guard zealously the interests of the tradition because it can be easily compromised. Fortified with Jewishness as their primary identification, and with an educated grasp of Judaic values and ideals, families may then face the importunities of secularism and negotiate the tensions that emanate from the encounter.

Chapter 4

# THE PASSAGE FROM CHILDHOOD
# TO ADULTHOOD

In chapters II and III, which dealt with authority and independence in parent-child relationships, the focus was not on the adolescent, but on the parent-child system. As the "significant other" in the parent-child developmental crisis, the modern adolescent passes through a critical stage of transition from childhood to adulthood. There is a vast social science and popular literature that contributes to our understanding of this phenomenon and guides parents and professionals in dealing with the problems of the adolescent years. There is, however, a paucity of available literature on Judaism's views of adolescence and the critical issues facing the young person.

This chapter explores Judaism's conception of adolescence, the needs of this age-group vis-a-vis the interests of the Jewish community, and some similarities and differences between Judaic, psychological, and anthropological perspectives of this status passage. Issues facing the modern Jewish adolescent are compared with those of his or her historical counterpart.

Several questions have helped to focus this study:

1. Does Judaism conceive of the passage from childhood to adulthood as occurring in several stages, or in a direct movement from one to the other?
2. Does Judaism consider adolescence to be a distinct period of life, or is it part of adulthood?
3. What are the functions and meanings of the ritual of passage?
4. What are the tasks and the problems of the adolescent in the traditional Jewish community and in modern society?

## STAGES IN THE PASSAGE FROM CHILDHOOD TO ADULTHOOD

In Judaism the actual line of demarcation between the stage of childhood and adulthood is thirteen years for a boy and twelve years for a girl. There are, however, several stages through which the boy passes before reaching the age of majority, and several thereafter, until he becomes independent from his parents. The girl passes through one stage before and one stage after reaching majority.

The stages of childhood and adulthood are defined by Judaism in legal terms, i.e., the obligations of parents and the legal validity of children's acts. There is recognition that with the child's growing maturity, the obligations upon the parents increase, and the child's actions and transactions assume greater legal validity.

### Childhood

The first stage is that of *katan*—minor. The *katan* is described as one without *da'at*—knowledge and sense—thus his actions possess no legal validity. If he performs a *mitzvah*, it is considered invalid. For example, if he slaughters an animal on his own—*shekhitah*—the meat may not be eaten. The status of *katan* technically exists until the age of thirteen when the child becomes a *gadol*—grown—but as he moves through childhood, many more of his actions become legally valid. The Talmud delineates the stages of the life cycle in terms of their tasks and characteristics.

> He used to say: at five years (the age is reached) for the study of Scriptures, at ten for (the study of) the Mishna, at thirteen for the mitzvoth, at fifteen for (the study of) the Gemarah, at eighteen for marriage, at twenty for the pursuit of the aim (in life)...(Avot V, 25).

The father is expected to teach his son Torah and prayer from the time he learns to speak (Sukah 42a), but normal study of Torah begins at the age of five, the entry into school. This continues for five years until, at the age of ten, the boy is introduced to Mishnah, the part of the Talmud codified by Rabbi Judah the Prince in the year 200. The study of Mishnah requires more logical reasoning and a greater breadth of understanding—cognitive tasks that the ten-year old can handle.

With reference to the performance of *mitzvot*, the Talmud states:

> Our Rabbis taught: a *katan* who knows how to shake a *lulav* (palmbranch) is obligated to do so; to wear *tzitzit* (fringes) is obligated to wear them; to take care of *tefillin* (phylacteries) his father buys *tefillin* for him...(Sukah 42a).

The age is not specified but it may be assumed that it begins after age five and intensifies by age ten. Nowadays many fathers buy a *lulav* and *etrog* (citron) for their young children, and boys also wear *tzitzit* at a young age. *Tefillin* are generally not worn until a month or so prior to *bar mitzvah*. Though these ritual acts are not considered legally valid, they are valuable preparations for the time when the boy will be legally obligated to perform them. Both positive and negative *mitzvot* fall within the teaching function of the father. Just as he is obligated to teach his son how to perform positive *mitzvot—lulav, tzitzit*, etc.—so it is incumbent upon him to restrain him from violating negative *mitzvot*. Even though the child, as a minor, is not culpable, the father is enjoined from sanctioning his deviant behavior (Rashi, Exodus 20:10). Thus, through the father's teaching, the *Halakhah* sought to ensure superego development in the child, and his eventual socialization into the Jewish community.

It is noteworthy that the age between five and eleven corresponds to what Freud called latency. Freud postulated that a biological reduction of libidinal drives or their effective repression permitted a relative calm in this period of transition between the Oedipal period and the onset of puberty. Lidz claims that there are important character traits that appear at this period in life, namely a sense of belonging, a sense of responsibility, and the quality of leadership. A sense of belonging refers to the assurance a child gains of being an accepted and integral part of the group and of the broader society. It entails an identification with the society in which the child lives and a commitment to its values and ethics. A sense of responsibility involves a willingness and capacity to live up to the expectations one has aroused. Both lead to the quality of leadership. In finding their places among peers, children begin to assume their places in society (Lidz, 1976).

Psychoanalysts have pointed out that there are significant changes in the ego during latency. Such ego activities as perception, learning, memory, and thinking become more firmly consolidated in the conflict-free sphere of the ego. There are more stringent inner controls due to the ascendancy of the superego. They become apparent in the emergence of behavior and in attitudes which are motivated by logic and oriented toward values. This stage is characterized by the widening scope of social, intellectual, and motor proficiencies (Blos, 1962). There appears to be a correspondence between psychological descriptions of latency and the rabbis' understanding of this stage of development. The dormancy of the sexual drive affords the child the opportunity to develop different facets of his personality—the superego, the intellect, and the capacity for industry (Erikson, 1950). Similarly, Judaism recognizes the growing intellectual ability of latency-age children by adding Mishnah to their study of Scriptures, and their need to be industrious by granting them the opportunity to perform *mitzvot*. Torah study and *mitzvah* performance imbue a feeling of belonging to the Jewish community, a sense of responsibility to live up to the moral expectations of parents and teachers, and leadership potential through intellectual and spiritual development.

In sum, Judaism viewed the latency stage of life as critical for socializing the child to Jewish values, norms, and community. Obligations were placed upon the parents and the schools, the two major social institutions with educational functions. During the age when sexual impulses were dormant and the child needed to develop what Erikson called "a sense of industry," the tradition sought to capitalize on the child's capacity for learning and doing by encouraging him to add Mishnah to his study of Scriptures, and to perform *mitzvot* that bring joy and satisfaction in their performance.

One of the major challenges facing the modern Jewish community is to improve the quality of Jewish education for the pre-*bar-mitzvah* age group, and to motivate more parents to educate their children Judaically. Only a minority of Jewish children attend Jewish schools (Sundays, afternoons, day schools). The recent adoption by federations throughout the United States and Canada of the principle that the support of

Jewish education is a *communal* responsibility, and not just one of the *religious* groups, augurs well for an increase in funding that would facilitate the hiring of qualified teachers. With reference to the curriculum, a contemporary approach to teaching Judaism needs to embrace both tradition and modernity. Its educational philosophy must affirm that "Judaism addresses the entire personality of the Jew, not merely his will. Hence the personality of the Jew, his inner world of thought and feeling, and his world of human relationships are primary objects of religious concern. *Mitzvot* seek to influence and change both these worlds (Jerusalem Seminar Series, 1980)."

In order for the modern Jewish family—both parents and children—to be motivated to pursue a Jewish education, it has to speak to them in modern language and address the issues of the day from a traditional value base. For too many people Judaism is perceived as a collection of ancient rituals without application to institutional life—politics, economics, education, government, welfare, the military, etc. Judaism's messages in these areas have not been translated into a popular idiom, and are therefore not available to the majority of Jews.

We live in a learning society; adult education courses are offered in most institutes of higher learning. The Jewish community needs to offer courses that would help adults understand political crises, military confrontations, inflation, medical ethics, marital relations, psychological dependency, relating to aged parents, the dependence-independence conflict of children, modern sex ethics, Jew-non-Jew relations, and many more concerns of educated adults. If parents can be turned on to Jewish learning, their homes will be alive with Jewish ideas. They will, in turn, motivate their children. The family will then enter a new phase of development: striving to live a deeply meaningful Jewish life in an open, secular society.

## Preadolescence

After the ages of five and ten, which demarcate two stages in the cognitive development and formal education of children, Judaism positioned a third stage immediately preceding the passage into adulthood, and granted it a more potent legal status than that of the earlier stages. Designated as *mufla ha-samukh l'ish,* this stage addresses boys at the age of twelve and girls at eleven. Their vows, and the things they buy and sell are considered legally valid. They are also urged to fast on the Day of Atonement and Tisha B'av.

The term *mufla ha-samukh l'ish* has been translated in different ways. Rashi comments that the word *mufla* derives from *l'hafli* which refers to the ability to express oneself clearly in words and to make vows (Rashi, Nazir 29b). Jastrow describes the child in this stage as one "whose power of discrimination is uncertain," "a doubtful person next to a man, i.e., a boy near the age of religious majority (Jastrow, 1950 p. 746)." He derives this meaning from the root, *Yi-palei*—unclear, uncertain; the boy is in the process of transition from one status to another.

In the psychological literature, the age of twelve for boys and eleven for girls is designated as preadolescence. It is the time for reawakened instinctual urges due in large measure to physical changes in bodily development. Concomitant with the surfacing of sexual feelings are changes in relations between the sexes, relationships with parents, renunciation of Oedipal wishes, and changes in self-image. It is the age of puberty, the first menarche, though puberty cannot be clearly located in a particular year of life (Blos, 1962). In addition to having to cope with sexual turmoil, the early adolescent must redirect affections and attachments away from the family toward the world. The young person is therefore more inclined to look to teachers and counselors for guidance in formulating moral principles.

In traditional Judaism, children at this stage are not described in terms of their biological development, sexual urges, peer and parent relations, or psychology. The rabbis were aware of the biological changes occurring in the child, but their major interest lay elsewhere. The process of physical development and maturational growth was acknowledged in terms of moral responsibility. The rabbis asked such questions as, What expectations can be placed upon the child approaching majority? Which of the preadolescent's acts can now be legally sanctioned because they are performed with conscious intent? The rabbis were concerned with the child's ability to perform actions with reason and intentionality.

The year before majority is the time of anticipatory socialization. The child looks forward to the day of formal leavetaking of childhood and joining the adult ranks. In the traditional as well as the modern Jewish family, it is the onset of the preparation for *bar mitzvah*, which is typically perceived as a privilege and an honor. Studying for the ceremonial separates the youth from younger children and encourages anticipation of the new status.

## The Age of Passage

In passing from childhood to adulthood, the thirteen year-old boy is called *ish*—man—and the twelve year-old girl, *na-arah*—young woman. Becoming a man/young woman involves the performance of *mitzvot,* and being formally held responsible for one's actions. The actual designation of these respective ages for boys and girls is a *halakhah l'Moshe mi-Sinai*—Moses' law from Sinai, thus a binding tradition not accompanied by any specific reason. By contrast, in Western culture there is no societal agreement as to the age at which an individual ceases to be a child (Blos, 1962).

The new status and role that Judaism assigns to the boy are portrayed in practical, poetic, and mystical images. Practically speaking, the boy is called *ish*—man—and *gadol*—grown—whose sense—*da'at*—and cognitive ability—*mahk-shava*—are now recognized. Poetic and mystical images portray him as a newborn, "the day of the *bar-mitzvah* is like the day of birth;" as one who is surrounded by angels when he does the *mitzvot;* as a person who, on the day of his *bar-mitzvah*, completes his spiritual endowment. Psychologically, he "stands in his own domain," and becomes independent of his parents. Socially, he joins the adult community of Israel and assumes responsibility for his fellow Jews. Taken together, these are the attributes of an adult in the Jewish community (Adler, 1977).

There are some slight variations for girls. They are not bound by all the *mitzvot,* for women are excluded from those that are time-bound (Kiddushin 29a), and they gain independence from parents at the age of *bogeret* (Kiddushin 3b)—twelve and a half. There were no *bat-mitzvah* ceremonies in olden days, and girls were not given a formal Jewish education. The focus was on boys; but girls, upon reaching the age of twelve, equally assumed legal responsibility for their actions.

The new status has positive effects for the adolescent and the community. It offers the adolescent a self-image which is definite, reciprocal, and group-bound; at the same time, the societal integration of the maturing child is promoted. Without this kind of environmental complementation or reinforcement, the adolescent's self-image loses clarity and cohesiveness (Blos, 1962). The model provided by Jewish society achieved this dual purpose: the adolescent's development of a secure Jewish identity, and integration into the Jewish community.

## Beyond the Age of Passage

After the age of passage, there are two additional statuses

and one intervening age-specific task that characterize adolescence. Though they achieve the status of *gadol*—grown—the adolescent boy and girl continue to be dependent on their parents, as they are not old enough to marry. Their dependency places them into a new legal category, *ben ha-somekh al shulkhan aviv*—the grown son who "depends" on his father's table, i.e., he lives in his parents' house and relies on their sustenance. According to Jewish law, the lost object that he finds and the salary that he earns belong to his father in exchange for his economic support (Hoshen Mishpat 270, 2). The child was not economically independent during adolescence as long as he was supported by his parents. Whether parents actually took his earnings is not the issue; the law gave them the right of access to them. The practical decision was probably determined by the family's economic status. In working-class Jewish families, children contribute to the family income from their part-time jobs. In middle-class Jewish families, children are encouraged to keep their income and not turn it over to their parents. Parents view this as an indication of their children's initiative toward independence.

The age-specific task that coincides with the status of the "grown son at his father's table," is the study of *gemara*—Talmud—at age fifteen (Avot V, 25). Having spent 5 years in the study of the *Mishnah* (which began at age ten) no subject contained in the *gemara* is foreign to the young man. By this time he is able to follow all the debates in the *gemara* with full comprehension, and to grasp their conclusions with ease (Hirsch, 1969, p. 507).

The age of fifteen for the study of *gemara* corresponds to the age of what Piaget calls "formal operations." As Erikson explains it, "the youth can now operate on hypothetical propositions, can think of possible variables and potential relations, and think of them in thought alone, independent of certain concrete checks previously necessary. As Jerome S. Bruner puts it, the child now can conjure up systematically the full range of alternative possibilities that could exist at any given time (Erikson, 1963, p.11)."

These cognitive abilities are required for the study of *gemara* and are simultaneously developed through such study. Talmud study sharpens one's thinking and inferential capacities on various levels of abstraction. The fifteen year-old boy is deemed ready to engage in this intellectual venture.

In day schools and *yeshivot* today, *gemara* is taught at a much earlier age, around eleven years. Regardless of the merits of this practice, it is obvious that the child's comprehension at that age is vastly inferior to the understanding and the readiness at age fifteen. Apparently the rabbis designated the latter age as the onset for Talmud study because they knew that the boy could approach it with a serious, curious attitude, and with an extensive background of 10 years of textual analysis.

The second status during the teen years, after Talmud study, is attained at eighteen, *ben shemoneh esrai l'hupah*—the age of marriage (Avot V, 25). It is assumed that the young man is not dependent on his parents for economic support. Upon marriage he leaves his parents' house and sets up his own. It is the formal age of independence. Marriage can be undertaken prior to age eighteen and of course, later, but not too much later, for after twenty, the *Yetzer hara*—evil inclination— an alias for the sexual impulse—will have become dominant in the young man's life and difficult to control (Kiddushin 29b).

For all intents and purposes, adolescence in Judaism terminates at the age of marriage, ideally at age eighteen. Economic independence, geographical distance from parents, and psychological self-sufficiency coincide to warrant the designation of *ish* and *gadol* on the young man. He is now fully a man.

With entry into marriage, the numerous statuses of the individual's passage from childhood to adulthood have been traversed. A total of six stages were discerned that encompassed educational, biological, intellectual, moral, and behavioral components in varying degrees of interrelationship.

Formal education begins at the age of five, more advanced education at age ten, along with the opportunity to do *mitzvot*. With the termination of latency, the period of puberty—age twelve for boys and eleven for girls—places the child in an anomalous legal status. The actual passage into adult status occurs a year thereafter. Since they are still dependent on their parents, their legal status is not that of an independent person. Cognitive abilities are recognized and encouraged at age fifteen through the study of Talmud, and total independence is achieved at age eighteen, the preferred age for marriage.

## ADOLESCENCE AS A DISTINCT PERIOD OF LIFE

It should be apparent from the foregoing discussion that adolescence in Judaism does not appear to constitute a distinct period of development, but is part of adulthood. In essence, there are two major stages of life: childhood and adulthood. The former terminates at age thirteen, when the latter begins. To be sure, there are developmental stages in childhood, even as there are in adulthood (Avot V, 25); but the reason for the sharp demarcation at thirteen for a boy and twelve for a girl is due to Judaism's proclivity for stressing behavior over psychology, and responsibility over identity.

The differences between childhood and adulthood are located in these areas. The child is not deemed responsible for his behavior, so the norms are not obligatory. The adult can be held responsible, so many more obligations devolve upon the grown person. To be an adult in Judaism is to be defined by one's acts; to be a responsible adult is to be held accountable for the consequences of one's acts.

One can discern Judaism's awareness of the psychology of status passage from its normative prescriptions. It was not necessary to spell out the stress and identity issues because they would not change the child's legal status. The child's degree of maturity is measured by the rationality and intentionality behind his or her actions. However, regardless of precociousness, the child formally becomes a *gadol* only upon reaching the specified age. Then he or she joins the adult community and must abide by the same religious norms as they do. The rabbis, however, distinguish between the adolescent's culpability by the human court and the heavenly court. The human court can mete out punishment for infractions of biblical laws under its jurisdiction. But the heavenly court does not mete out punishment for infractions committed against laws under its jurisdiction until the age of 20, regardless of the individual's marital status (Yalkut Shimoni, Gen. 5:1). The moratorium on punishment by the heavenly court was designed to foster a greater psychological readiness to assume adult responsibilities later on, and a deeper awareness of one's place in the community. It functioned as a breather for young adolescents who did not possess sufficient insights into their actions. It afforded them the freedom to utilize these years for growth and development, without the fear of God's punishment. It served to delay their full-fledged participation in the adult community and to legitimate their moral and religious inexperience in certain categories of behavior.

Thus the notion of the moratorium on divine punishment modifies the previous portrayal of adolescence as an integral part of adulthood. Adolescence is now viewed as oriented toward adulthood but partially distinct from it. It is essentially a transitional stage that possesses characteristics of childhood (nonculpability in certain categories of behavior) and adulthood (normative expectations). As the adolescent feels himself to be "inbetween," so does Judaism regard him.

In contrast to premodern societies, contemporary Western culture is witness to a rather recent phenomenon within the last 50 years—the emergence of the youth culture. Youth culture extends into graduate school and professional training, though it is most prominent during the teen years. It is not merely an apprenticeship to the skills of adulthood, but it has roles, values, sexual attractiveness, immediate pleasure, and friendship in a way that is true neither of childhood nor of adulthood. The youth culture is not always antiadult, but it is belligerently nonadult. It is an expression of the reluctance of many young men and women to face the unknown perils of adulthood.

The youth culture is partially a consequence of the discontinuity between age groups—childhood and adulthood—and not only reflective of the increasing gap between the generations—parents and children. "Generational discontinuities are gaps in time between one mature generation and the next; but age group discontinuities are gaps between different age groups at the *same* time... Thus, the youth culture provides a kind of way-station, a temporary stopover in which one can muster strength for the next harrowing stage of the trip (Keniston, 1963, pp. 176-7)."

One of the positive functions of the youth culture is what Erikson characterizes as a psychosocial moratorium on adulthood—a stage which provides young people with an opportunity to develop their identity as adults. The function of the moratorium is to alleviate pressure on youth to grow up quickly, to take on adult responsibilities, values, and roles. It provides time for the setting in of the transition from childhood, for developing a keener self-awareness, and a sorting out of options and opportunities for career goals, heterosexual relationships and value selection. These positive functions are necessary in a society where adulthood, i.e., economic self-sufficency, marriage, and communal responsibility, is psychologically distant from the adolescent.

Jewish adolescents today are very much integrated into contemporary culture and distant from traditional Jewish culture. They are teenagers like the others and participate in the youth culture as they do. They do not consider themselves adults, even though they may have been *bar-* or *bat-mitzvahed.* Consequently they do not feel compelled to take on the roles and responsibilities of adults, but, instead, opt to take advantage of the psychosocial moratorium with a minimum of obligation and a maximum of freedom.

Parents and professionals may find it instructive to engage adolescents in discussion on topics that evoke similarities and differences between adolescents then and now. How does Judaism define this stage of life? What are its normative expectations of the adolescent? Did a youth culture exist in olden times? What is understood by moratorium? What was life like for the Jewish adolescent of old, as compared with today? The Judaic notions of stages, obligations, cognitive development, and moratorium seem to coincide with current conceptions of adolescence. Judaism can offer insights into this stage of life that may assist the adolescent, parents, and professionals to cope with the transition from childhood more effectively.

## FUNCTIONS AND MEANINGS OF THE RITUAL OF PASSAGE

The rite of passage from childhood to adulthood is not a category limited to Judaism; it is an almost universal phenomenon whose study provides a cross-cultural perspective for understanding Judaism's approach.

Ages regarding the onset of adolescence vary among those cultures that have made the most of this rite of passage. It is, therefore, a misnomer to think of puberty in biological terms; the ceremonies are a recognition of the child's new social status of adulthood. Ruth Benedict (1954) states:

> In order to understand puberty institutions, we do not need most analyses of the necessary nature of *rites de passage*; we need rather to know what is identified in different cultures with the beginning of adulthood and their methods of admitting to a new status. Not biological puberty, but what adulthood means in that culture conditions the puberty ceremony (p. 23).

Different initiation ceremonies reflect different definitions of adulthood. In a society where adulthood means warfare, the youth's strength and courage will be tested through severe physical challenges of endurance. In a society where adulthood means participation in a male cult which excludes women, puberty ceremonies are symbolic repudiations of the bonds with the female sex (Benedict, 1954).

Initiation ceremonies emphasize a social fact: the adult prerogatives of men are more far-reaching than women's in every culture. Consequently it is more common for societies to take note of this period in boys than in girls. The adolescence of girls may be a theme which a culture does not institutionalize. Margaret Mead discovered that a girl's puberty in Samoa falls in a particularly unstressed and peaceful period during which no adolescent conflicts manifest themselves. Adolescence, therefore, may not only be culturally passed over without ceremonial; it may also be without importance in the emotional life of the girl and in the attitude of the village toward her (Mead, 1956).

Another reason advanced for the predominance of male initiation rites is their relation to sex identity conflict. When conditions for sex identity are confusing due to early relationships with the mother in patrilocal societies, the rite at adolescence seems to force the boy to relinquish his unacceptable female identification and to identify once and for all with his male initiators. American society, which is not characterized by conditions which foster sex identity conflict, does not practice initiation ceremonies (Brown, 1963).

In Judaism, the male initiation rite into adolescence is the *bar mitzvah*. Until recent times, only the boy was initiated; there was no ceremony for the girl. This practice seems to be consistent with the pattern found in many societies. As Judaism is a male-dominated religion, in which all the *mitzvot* are incumbent upon the male and far fewer upon the female, it emphasizes the entry of the boy into male society. He was to begin formal Jewish education at an early age and continue it throughout his lifetime. At the age of thirteen he is to take full responsibility for fulfilling the commandments. Through study and practice he is prepared to enter into the adult community. The actual ceremonial of the *bar mitzvah* takes place in the synagogue, usually on the Sabbath, when the boy is called to the Torah to recite the blessings. Those who can, also read the *haftorah*—the portion from the Prophets. More educationally advanced students may also lead the services. Most bar mitzvah ceremonies are followed by a festive meal.

There are some highly valued traditions associated with the *bar mitzvah* festivities.

> It is a *mitzvah* for the father to make a *seudah*—festive meal—on the day his son becomes a *bar mitzvah*, as on the day he marries. And there is no greater meal than this, for they give praise and thanks to God that the son has achieved the rank of *gadol*—grown—who is now commanded to perform *mitzvot*, and that the father has merited to raise him until now and to enter him into the covenant of the Torah (Adler, 1977, p. 67).

The tradition of the *bar mitzvah seudah* dates back to the time of Abraham who prepared a big *seudah* on the day that Isaac became thirteen (Gen. 21:8). It is also recorded that R. Simeon bar Yohai gave a big festive meal on the occasion of the *bar mitzvah* of his son, R. Elazar (Zohar, Genesis 11:1).

The child's entry into the Jewish community is highlighted by several significant customs. There was a practice in Jerusalem that the father of the *bar mitzvah* would bring his son before every elder to bless the boy and pray for him to succeed in Torah studies and good deeds (Adler, p. 73). The highly respected elders represented continuity of the tradition and the community. Their blessings were a symbolic gesture of their acceptance of the *bar mitzvah* into their ranks.

Other customs with symbolic meanings also confirmed the boy's new status. In many cities and towns, the *bar mitzvah* would give a learned discourse in some aspect of the Torah during the festive meal (p. 73). This signified an important change in his status and role. Whereas the boy had always been a student, a child who typically learns from teachers, on the day of his *bar mitzvah* he becomes a teacher, an adult. He is given an opportunity to teach other adults. It is a moment of elation and triumph. The *bar mitzvah* is also accorded the honor of leading the grace after the meal (p. 73). This, too, symbolizes his coming of age, his assumption of a new status through a religious ceremonial, an opportunity to lead, and not just to follow. This is the day in which the boy is the center of attention, the star of the show.

For girls it was different. They were not educated formally, but learned their roles informally from their mothers at home. Like the girls in Samoa, Jewish girls simply took on more domestic responsibilities upon reaching their majority; their transition was neither traumatic nor prominent, and consequently did not require a ceremonial.

This difference no longer exists today. Girls as well as boys receive formal Jewish education, and *bat mitzvah* ceremonies are conducted by most Jewish families, even the traditionally observant. The reasons are eminently obvious. Families are not equipped to educate their children Judaically at home; they must rely on the educational network. Boys and girls grow up in assimilated neighborhoods in an open society where a Jewish education is indispensable for strengthening their Jewish identities. The feminist movement has enhanced women's status and equality with men; one of its effects is girls' demand for a similar ceremonial passage into the Jewish community.

Mortimer Ostow (1977) has described the *bar mitzvah* ceremony as an ''intellectualized puberty ordeal'' that is a challenge to the boy. The discipline required to master this challenge and the moral teachings associated with it comply with his need for a set of external controls to supplement his inner controls which have been threatened by instinctual energies.

The parents also experience an ordeal. It seems to them that they are being judged by the community as to whether they have succeeded in communicating to the child their Jewish identity and a willingness to accept responsibility to the community. It is, in fact, a *family* ordeal, in which parents and child have to work together to establish and maintain each one's position in the community. It tends to bind parents and child into a closer relation.

A private aspect of the parents' experience is the feeling that the bar mitzvah ceremony fulfills an obligation of the parent to his own parent. He feels as though he were again the bar mitzvah youngster answerable to his father, and by his son's performance, he is reminded of his continuing obligation to his parents. The physical presence of the grandparent and his participation in the ritual reinforces the sense of generational and communal continuity which the grandparents signify for the child in his earliest years (Ostow, p. 56).

While many Jewish leaders have been severely critical of the materialistic nature of the *bar mitzvah* ceremony and its lack of intellectual and moral content, Ostow insists that it should be recognized as an event that celebrates a Jewish religious achievement in the Jewish community. While it is important to purify Jewish community behavior of vulgarity, the need for competitiveness and display that attaches itself to a religious ceremony indicates the strength of the ceremony. "Divorcing communal competition altogether from significant religious ceremonies is probably not possible, and is of doubtful desirability (p. 56)." Ostow advocates choosing tutors for *bar mitzvah* children who will provide not only a sound education, but be able to establish a warm, friendly relationship and convey a sense of high personal idealism and commitment. It is an opportunity to influence the young person profoundly and enduringly.

In sum, the ritual of passage in the modern Jewish community symbolizes the *bar* and *bat mitzvah's* assumption of adult responsibilities and the continuity of tradition, though they may not identify with the deeper meanings of the ceremonial owing to their involvement in the youth culture. The traditional significance of *bar mitzvah* presents a challenge to parents and professionals: to help the adolescent develop moral values, assume responsibility for the consequences of one's actions, deepen study of the Jewish heritage and involvement with the community, and thereby strengthen identity as a Jew.

## THE TASKS OF THE ADOLESCENT

The contrast between traditional and modern society with regard to the tasks of the adolescent has been succinctly enunciated by Keniston. "Oversimplifying, we might say that socialization is the main problem in a society where there are known and stable roles for children to fit into; but in a rapidly changing society like ours, identity formation increasingly replaces socialization in importance (Keniston, 1963, p. 178)." The socialization function belongs primarily to the adult, and it is the child who is socialized; identity formation is primarily the task of the child, though adults are instrumental in the process.

The distinction between the socialization function and identity formation affords important insights into the differential tasks of the adolescent in traditional and modern societies, and the problems of the modern Jewish adolescent. In traditional Jewish society the major responsibility for socializing the child into Jewish tradition and community devolved upon parents, teachers, and elders. The noblest task and the most important communal function of any adult was teaching Torah to the young. Education was a supreme value, and Jews took their responsibility to educate very seriously.

The task of the adolescent girl was to receive the tradition from her mother and internalize it through practice. Though her role was domestically oriented, she still needed to be thoroughly educated in the laws and traditions in order eventually to transmit them to her children.

The task of the adolescent boy was to receive the tradition from his elders and make his unique contribution as he accrues greater knowledge and analytic skills. Throughout his youth, he was the student who was expected to listen, learn, and challenge the ideas of his teachers. He was not a passive recipient of knowledge, but an active participant in the learning process. This process sharpened his mind and enabled him eventually to create his own *hidushim*—new interpretations of the tradition.

Identity, therefore, was not an issue. The adolescent knew who he was and what was expected of him, for the goals of the socialization process were brought home to him throughout the developmental stages of his youth. The adolescent's search for meaning took place within a heavily institutionalized society that provided an ideological framework of morals, values, and ideals. He was not thrown back upon his own powers to choose among alternatives but was taught the one and right way, to which he could later add his own interpretations. When he was ready to embody the social and cultural values of the Jewish community in his actions, the socialization was deemed to have been effective.

The Jewish adolescent acquired a sense of time and history from his studies and ritual experiences. He lived the tradition. Tradition, in the words of T.S. Eliot (1963), involves the historical sense, which in turn, involves "a perception, not only of the pastness of the past, but of its presence; . . . a sense of the timeless as well as of the temporal and of the timeless and of the temporal together. . .(p. 14)." Soloveitchik (1965) captures this theme when he describes the experience of the traditional Jew.

> The *Masorah* (traditional) community cuts across the centuries, indeed millennia, of calendric time and unites those who already played their part, delivered their message, acquired fame and withdrew from the covenantal stage quietly and humbly with those who have not yet been given the opportunity to appear on the covenantal stage and who wait for their turn in the anonymity of the

"about to be." Thus the individual member of the covenantal faith community feels rooted in the past and related to the future. The "before" and the "after" are interwoven in his time experience... He is no longer an
evanescent being; he is rooted in everlasting time, in
eternity itself (p. 47).

The Jewish adolescent experienced this time awareness,
for it pervaded traditional Jewish living. He was aided by the
Jewish calendar which constantly renewed the past in the
present by reminding the Jew that a festival is coming, an
historic event that requires preparation in order to maximize its
meaning. The adolescent, then, lived in the reality of the
present, but incorporated into it a sense of closeness with the
past and an anticipation of the future.

In modern society, the major task of adolescence is
identity formation. Erikson's conception of identity helps us to
understand the challenges confronting the modern adolescent
more precisely. Identity refers to a sense of sameness, a unity of
personality felt by the individual and recognized by others as
having consistency in time—of being an irreversible historical
fact.

Every human being develops during adolescence what
Erikson (1963) calls an "historical perspective." "It is a sense
of the irreversibility of significant events and an often urgent
need to understand fully and quickly what kind of happenings
in reality and thought determine others, and why...Youth,
therefore, is sensitive to any suggestion that it may be hope-
lessly determined by what went before in life histories or in
history (p. 12)." The adolescent is sensitive to any suggestion
that identity is historically predetermined. For this reason, he
or she often rejects parents and authorities, in the search for
individuals and movements that claim that they can get ahead
of the future by predicting it. Thus adolescents will not be
bound by the past, but take their chances in preparing for the
future.

Erikson expresses the tensions between the young and the old in a lyrical statement.

To enter history, each generation of youth must find an identity consonant with its own childhood and consonant with an ideological promise in the perceptible historical process. But in youth the tables of childhood dependence begin slowly to turn: no longer is it merely for the old to teach the young the meaning of life, whether individual or collective. It is the young who, by their responses and actions, tell the old whether life as represented by the old and as presented to the young has meaning; and it is the young who carry in them the power to confirm those who confirm them and, joining the issues, to renew and to regenerate, or to reform and to rebel (p. 20).

One aspect of the psychology of rapid change is the discontinuity between the generations. When the generational past becomes ever more distant and the future more predictable, the sense of sameness that is the hallmark of identity becomes elusive. More work and creative efforts are required to attain it. Youth tends not to listen to the old, as testified by the absence of paternal exemplars in many contemporary plays, novels, and films. As the past becomes more remote psychologically, there is a greater tendency to disregard it altogether. The extreme form of this trend is found in the "now" generation's emphasis on present satisfactions, with an almost total refusal to consider future consequences or past commitments. Here the future and the past disappear completely and a greater intensification of the present is sought (Keniston, p. 174).

Developing a sense of continuity and history is only one of the adolescent's tasks in the struggle to form an identity. Another task of identity formation is the development of an ideology, a philosophy of life, a basic outlook on the world with which to orient one's actions as an adult.

In an ideologically stable society, which despite their wanderings and exile could characterize Jewish society throughout history, the Jewish adolescent received the ideology from his elders as part of the socialization process. The ideology was not pluralistic, but rather unidimensional, though the adolescent was aware of other points of view. Other ideologies, particularly if they conflicted with the one transmitted to him, tended to be devalued. One might say that the adolescent underwent an indoctrination process in order to ensure his internalization of the particular ideology espoused by his parents and teachers. The same pattern obtains today in the so-called "yeshiva world."

In modern society, a time of rapid ideological change, it seldom suffices for a young person simply to accept some ideology from the past. The task today is more difficult; it involves selecting from many ideologies those elements which are most relevant and enduring. This achievement takes time, and for the talented, it takes a long time until they can assimilate various ideologies and form their own. This demands a high degree of intelligence, the support of a significant group, curiosity and initiative. It also requires the ability to live with the tensions of uncertainty. —a tall order for the adolescent living amidst changing values and mores.

Modern Jewish adolescents live in such a society. They are part of the mainstream of the youth culture, seeking their identity and sorting out ideologies along with their peers, but with one difference—their Jewishness. The fact that they are Jewish provides them with both a burden and an opportunity. The burden consists of the need to digest the identities and ideologies from the past, which in their original forms do not really engage the modern mind because of the difference in language and culture. Jewish youth have an opportunity to translate the language and culture of the past into the present in order to open up a universe of discourse with history.

The problem is that today's Jewish adolescents are not concerned with history. They too, would prefer to live in the present, with all its uncertainty. The uncertainty of the present fosters discomfort, but to adopt the certainty of Jewish faith, practice, and history is not an enticing option. This is because the Judaism of the past is conceived to be unidimensional, rigid, obsolete, authoritarian, and intolerant of difference. The time has come to rid ourselves of these misconceptions. The educated Jewish adolescent would be receptive to ideas from the tradition that can speak to him or her in a shared language. It is the responsibility of Jewish educators to create this language in order to apply ideas and values that possess contemporary meaning.

The ideas and values from the tradition must address the private concerns of the students. Heschel (1967) insisted that "you can affect a person only if you reach his inner life, the level where every human being is insecure and feels his incompleteness, the level of awareness that lies beyond articulation (p. 58)." Jewish educators are recognizing the need to evoke the inner conflicts of the students and enable them to talk about their fears and anxieties in the classroom. They realize that Jewish education is not merely the imparting of information or the clarification of values, but the interface between them: the transmission of values from the tradition that interact with the values of the students. The task of the teacher is to mediate between the tradition's perspective and the students' concerns.

As an example, one of the difficulties of the modern human condition entails living with uncertainty in a world of change and revolution. Does Judaism have anything to say on the subject that can enlighten one's thinking? Can it help the modern adolescent to deal with the multiplicity of choices, and the self-doubts that prevent the attainment of certainty and sameness? Hartman (1978) has developed an interpretation of traditional Judaism whose vocabulary includes such terms as struggle, risk, and uncertainty, the pain of doubt, the risk of failure. "Struggle is inherent in our world; that which brings forth good also spawns evil (p. 99)." Although the world is unpredictable and dangerous, we Jews are bidden to live in it. "Therefore choose life" means give birth to children, build synagogues, schools, and communities. The *Halakhah* requires that we transform our beliefs and ideals into action. But this always entails the risk of failure. Many of our most important decisions are made without guarantees about their outcome. "When one marries, does one know how long it will last? When one has a child, can one foresee the future? (P. 256)" Hartman's faith "affirms the inescapability of risks. . . . To wish to create a world without risks is to wish for a kind of existence which heaven cannot grant (p. 99)." And again, "The path of *Halakhah* is fraught with risks and uncertainties. This, however, is the adventure of living by a Torah that is 'not in heaven' (p. 125)."

In order to attract modern Jewish adolescents to Jewish living and to the Jewish community, we need to address their concerns in a language that they can understand. They need to know that their life struggles, which they deem to be unique to themselves, have been the struggles of Jews through the millennia, that the uncertainty of their lives, their doubts about God, miracles, and Israel's election, the awkwardness of their marginality and difference, the meaning of being a Jew in an age of universalism and equality, the guilt and self-doubt in coming to terms with one's sexuality—have perplexed Jews before, and each had to deal with these issues in one's own way, assisted by the laws and values of the tradition.

Adolescents who reject Judaism do so partly because its ideology is either not transmitted or transmitted intact from the past. Though the ideology is not anachronistic, its language is. The challenge of revamping the language of Jewish education is enormous. It requires a cadre of talented educators who are not afraid of delving into the tradition to search out the unusual, the lone voice, the rebel, the pulls and the tensions in problem situations, the risks, partial successes, and failures of human attempts to create a just society. The Torah does speak to modern people, but it is a coded language until we use the intellectual tools at our discretion to decipher the code and create a vocabulary of renewal and inspiration.

## THE PROBLEMS OF THE ADOLESCENT

Adolescents in the traditional Jewish community and in modern society face two major developmental problems: sexuality, and relationship with parents. These have been selected for explication because they are equally prominent in both societies, whereas problems related to peer group relationships, for example, do not appear in the traditional literature.

### Sexuality

In Judaism there are two indices of attaining majority: chronological age, and the appearance of pubic hair. Maimonides (1956, Laws of Marriage II, 1) states that the thirteen year-old boy and twelve year-old girl are not considered adults until they show physical signs of puberty. However, the Code of Jewish Law, subsequent to Maimonides, accepts age in years as the sufficient index; the appearance of pubic hair is not investigated (Rama, Shulkhan Arukh, Orach Haim 55:5). Regardless of the actual appearance of pubertal signs, Judaism was well aware of the bodily changes that occur during this period of life, and their correspondence with awakened sexual urges. The rabbis were wont to designate instinctual drives as the *yetzer hara*—the evil impulse; not that they were evil in and of themselves, for they were part of the human condition, but their overindulgence could lead to deviation from the moral life (Linzer 1978; "Evil Impulse", 1981). The *yetzer hara* enters the child at birth; hence its equation with the instincts, the id impulses and egocentricity. The *yetzer hatov*—the good impulse—enters the child at age thirteen (The Fathers According to Rabbi Nathan, 16). It is equated with moral responsibility, concern for the needs of others, and the sublimation of the *yetzer hara* for socially constructive ends. (Montefiore and Loewe, 1963). Judaism believed that when a child attains the age of majority he has the capacity to transform the instinctual impulses indwelling from birth into socially acceptable modes of behavior.

Penetrating the surface definition of this dual inclination in man, one can readily discern the perennial conflict that must perforce exist prior to the execution of human action. Each inclination vies for supremacy over the ego, and it is the ego that must negotiate their conflict and emerge with a clear sense of direction. This is a very difficult task for the adolescent, because the instinctual, sexual drives, which are so powerful, seek discharge.

The question that faced the rabbis was how to help the adolescent boy to cope with his *yetzer hara* in a way that is morally responsible and does not violate Judaic norms. They confronted the problem squarely, and offered some very practical suggestions: early marriage, study of Torah, avoidance of the opposite sex, and discharge in a state of anonymity. These suggestions were offered to boys and not to girls because boys were deemed to have a stronger *yetzer hara*—in this case interpreted as the sexual drive—which needed control and sublimation. The *yetzer hara* in girls could be interpreted as egoecentricity, rather than sexual impulses.

Early marriage, at age eighteen, did not really solve the problem for the fourteen and fifteen year-old, for they were deemed too young to assume family responsibilities. The younger boys' problem could be helped by the second suggestion, which was Torah study. The intensive intellectual experience of studying *gemara* at age fifteen served to sublimate sexual instincts, as indicated by R. Ishmael: "My son, if this villian meets you, drag him into the house of study; if he is a stone he will melt, if he is metal he will explode (Sukah 52b)." Torah study has the power to destroy the *yetzer hara*.

Rava, a Talmudic rabbi, proposed another remedy: "It is an accepted fact that the *yetzer hara* becomes stronger from visual stimulation (Sotah 8a)." The implicit resolution of conflict is the separation of the sexes. It is for this reason that the sexes were separated in Jewish schools, in the synagogue, in public gatherings, and in private rooms.

A fourth remedy for defusing the sexual drive was proposed by R. Elaye Ha-zaken: "If a man feels his impulses dominating him, he should go to a place where no one recognizes him, dress in black clothing, and do as his heart desires—but let him not profane the name of heaven publicly (Hagiga 16a)." Here permission is apparently granted to discharge one's sexual impulses and not merely sublimate them as in the foregoing proposals. This is worded as a last resort, i.e., if all other efforts at sublimation fail, "if his impulses dominate him." It is a practical, but not preferable, approach. The other approaches are more esteemed because they appeal to the individual's striving for self-control.

In general, boys seem to experience urgency concerning sex sooner after puberty than girls, and they must find ways of coping with it. Genital sensations cause restlessness, direct the boy's thoughts to sexual objects, and urge him toward relief. According to Lidz (1976) erections occur with greater frequency, heat, and even pain; and unexpected erections can cause embarrassment and feelings of shame which contribute to the frequency of blushing during this time of life.

Masturbation, widely practiced by most adolescent boys and girls, often provokes guilt and concern. Such feelings may derive from the fantasies that generally accompany the act, but also from the indications from adults and peers that it is shameful and harmful. Although the belief that masturbation causes impotence is no longer widespread, such an idea fades slowly, and masturbation continues to be a source of much anguish to many adolescents. Boys are more apt to be troubled than girls, perhaps because of the loss of semen. They struggle to overcome the urge for relief and gratification and to renounce the practice, and when they fail to fulfil their intentions, they suffer a loss of self-respect. Lidz claims that such concerns are usually weathered. There is also a positive function to masturbation. "...the ability to gain relief from sexual impulses through masturbation often permits the relative quiet needed for study or for delaying marriage in order to prepare for a career (p. 323)."

Masturbation is only one of the ways in which adolescents sublimate their sexual impulses. Athletic prowess is another, as the young person seeks to gain status among peers and to emulate heroes. Same-sex peers are more important at this stage, though daydreaming about the other sex appears at this time too. Religion also provides an outlet as adolescents seek values and ideals. "Adolescents now often experience a closeness to a Deity and feel that they have support and guidance in countering the temptations that are besetting them. The attachment to the church will form an indirect continuing bond to the parents, whom they may now be starting to deny (p. 329)."

The options available to the modern Jewish adolescent seem to incline more toward those enumerated by Lidz than those offered by the rabbis. Early marriage is not feasible, and the study of Torah can be considered mainly for the religiously inclined. In Israel, the proliferation of yeshivot for native Israelis as well as youth from abroad, particularly the United States, attests to the attraction of Torah study in the Jewish State, and the acceptable delay in forming serious heterosexual relationships. The separation of the sexes is not an option in public high schools, only in yeshivot. R. Elaye's remedy—discharging sexual impulses in a clandestine setting—is an option, but it is unclear whether he meant masturbation or coitus. Assuming that he sanctioned both, unlimited license should not be inferred, but it is rather to be a chance indulgence in a moment of weakness. Persistence of sexual discharge is not sanctioned by Judaism; sublimation is the preferred mode for dealing with libidinal pressures.

In counseling and educating Jewish adolescents concerning their sexual drives and conduct, it is incumbent upon parents and professionals not to stress the prohibitive aspects, but the normalcy of such impulses, the difficulty of controlling them, and the legitimacy of the conflicts they engender. The Jewish sex ethic can be invoked to reinforce the reality of the inner struggle, and the several options that are available to deal with it. To stress the repression of the sexual impulses is the wrong tactic, for it will inevitably lead to strong guilt feelings and rebellion against the ethic. A balanced view should be offered in which neither repression nor free expression is counseled, but rather the normalcy of drives and feelings and their channeling into constructive modes of behavior.

## Parent-Child Relationships

In chapter II, a Judaic model of the parent-child relationship was proposed that acknowledged the needs of parents to be respected and revered and the needs of the child to become independent. Since there were bound to be situations in which their respective needs clashed, the *Halakhah* saw fit to offer guidelines for resolving these conflicts. The situations that are recorded in the *Shulkhan Arukh*—Code of Jewish Law— (Yoreh Deah, 240) friendship, study and marriage—occur during adolescence while the child is still living in the parents' house. The legal decision in favor of the child acknowledges respect for the child's private sphere where developmental needs do not impinge on the parents' dignity. In these cases, the law does not describe the tensions and the emotional consequences of the conflict; it leaves it for the reader to create the scenario and the dialogue. It poses the conflict and renders the decision in order to guide the reader to a particular course of action.

The psychological literature on adolescence takes the opposite track. It describes the tensions and pulls between the adolescent and the parents, the dynamics underlying their conflicts, and different approaches toward their resolution. It does not *prescribe* as the religion does; it merely *describes* what typically occurs in families with adolescents. Many of those descriptions can be useful in developing an approach to the modern Jewish adolescent.

There are two aspects of the adolescent's perception of the parents that are particularly significant for this discussion. The crisis of adolescence occurs at the same time as a critical period in the parents' lives. Parents are facing middle age and the realization that their own lives have reached a climax in terms of what they will be able to achieve in life. Lidz (1976) portrays this contrast vividly:

> It may be of particular significance that the parents are coming to final terms with the limitations imposed by "the realities of life" just at the time when the adolescent offspring's imagination is beginning to soar and the adolescent is becoming impatient with the limitation that adults and their society impose by their stodginess and conservatism; the difference between the generations and the age-old ideologic conflict between them reach their zenith (p. 341).

The contrast between the falling comet of the parents and the rising star of the adolescent is stark. The child will be affected by how the parents as individuals and as a couple cope with the consequential problems in their lives. The young person's struggle for independence and the parents' efforts to maintain some modicum of control exacerbate the conflict between them. The child's attacks upon their character constitute a serious blow to the parents' authority and self-esteem.

A second aspect of the adolescent's perception of the parents provides a penetrating understanding of their relationship at this stage.

> At this developmental stage, when the oedipal resolution must be confirmed, and when the young person needs tangible models to follow into adulthood, who the parents are and how they interrelate is particularly important to their child's harmonious development. The adolescent is becoming aware of the parent as a real person and model rather than a fantasied image; and who the parent is influences whom the child seeks to become. The coalition between the parents, the support they give one another,

the admiration they have for one another greatly influence the youth's transition through the adolescent period (p. 339).

Here, Lidz stresses the quality of the marital relationship as a crucial influence on the adolescent's self-image and evolving identity. Conflicts between parents, lack of respect for one another, and the dearth of sharing and love create tension in the family and provide the adolescent with a negative image of parenthood. Contrariwise, when parents are attuned to each other's needs, share their interdependency as a mutual strength, respect what the other is, enable one another to develop themselves, and provide mutual support for their respective roles in the family, the child lives within a cohesive family unit which serves as a preferred model for a future family life.

The adolescent similarly observes the parents' aging process and is equally a keen witness to the quality of their relationship as husband and wife. The young person is also aware of their waning strength and their increasing dependency on their offspring, first for small chores and then for bigger ones—this, at the age when the adolescent is flexing the muscles and feeling strong and invincible. Judaism could help the young person to become more sensitive to the parents' physical and emotional needs, for the *mitzvah* of *kibbud*—honor—is addressed to children whose parents are aging. Parents can teach that to be dependent is human, to need another person is natural, and to respond to dependency is virtuous.

The Jewish adolescent's self-image and ideals can be buttressed not only by the authenticity of the parents' relationship as husband and wife but also by Jewish values in marriage. Love and honor are dominant themes, as are the expectations that the couple treat each other with deference and self-sacrifice (Maimonides 1956, Laws of Marriage, XV, 19, 20). These sound like old-fashioned values today, but they are still viable. It is very difficult for people to be real, to be honest with themselves and with each other, and to expose their essential selves to their children, who are the keenest observers of their parents' foibles and strengths. If parents want to exert an influence on their children's self-image and ideals, they need to be open with them and let them see them as they are. The family that lives a Jewish way of life can enrich the interaction and growth of its members through mutual respect and sensitivity to needs.

## Summary and Conclusions

This study has revealed that, in Judaism, childhood and adolescence are divided into several developmental stages. These stages are defined not by the psychology of the growth process, though it is implicit, but by normative requirements and the legal validity of acts. Judaism is concerned with obligations and acts, and whether the developing child could justify personal actions through intentionality and reason.

The age of majority—thirteen for a boy and twelve for a girl—provides a clear demarcation between the status and responsibilities of the child and those of the adult. Status passage, however, does not imply that the youth has become a full-fledged adult, for the young person is absolved from divine punishment until the age of twenty. The notion of moratorium leads to the conclusion that Judaism views the adolescent in transition, in some ways a child and in most others, an adult. Adolescence, then, is not a distinct period of life, as reflected in modern youth culture, but is primarily oriented toward the adult world of religious commitments and communal obligations.

Sex differences in the rite of passage in the traditional Jewish community seem to parallel other societies where different definitions of adulthood obtain. Since Judaism defines the male's role as commanding more religious responsibilities, it accentuates his passage ritual. In modern times, as the religious needs of girls assume greater prominence, religious rituals have been created for them to mark the significance of their status passage.

The two major tasks of the adolescent—identity formation and ideology acquisition—are more difficult to accomplish today than in the past. In the past, the adolescent's identity and ideology were provided by the parents and teachers through socialization into the Jewish tradition. The modern Jewish adolescent must form his or her own identity and formulate an ideology, as they are not generally now transmitted by those institutional representatives. The plurality of choices and the decline of traditional authority have an unsettling effect on the adolescent's decisions and lead to a state of uncertainty.

Two developmental problems of adolescence—coming to terms with sexuality and negotiating the authority-independence issue with parents—appear as problematic today as in the past, but for different reasons. In the traditional Jewish community, the outlets available for sublimating the adolescent's sexual drive were limited. Expression of sexuality—both verbal and physical—was repressed; avoidance of heterosexual contacts and intensive Torah study for the young adolescent boy were the preferred forms of sublimation. If the adolescent thought about sex or masturbated, the guilt feelings were overwhelming. There was no one to talk to about such feelings, because the subject was taboo. Early marriage for older adolescents was a necessary option for alleviating guilt and enabling their sexual impulses to be discharged in a religiously acceptable way.

The modern Jewish adolescent, by contrast, is exposed to a sexually permissive society. With more outlets for channeling normal tensions, the young person is less burdened with guilt and repression. The flexibility of limits and the plurality of choices, however, make it more difficult to impose self-restraints and to develop normative and moral guidelines for sexual behavior.

In the parent-child arena, the traditional Jewish adolescent willingly submitted to the parents' authority. Through this relationship with them, he or she developed an obedient personality to all authority figures. The personal need to strive for independence was circumscribed by the priority of the community's need to maintain the traditional authority system.

Parents in the modern Jewish family demand less obedience, and encourage more independence in their children. The adolescent gets the message that he or she must find the balance between respecting one's parents and meeting one's own developmental needs. As one's parents age and their strengths wane, they will require more of one's help and a greater affirmation of their dignity. By contrast, with early marriage and childbirth, parents of adolescents would not be aging but in the fulness of their powers. It is a difficult balance for the adolescent to maintain because the thrust for growth and self-reliance is bound to clash with the parents' expectations of service and deference.

Whether in the provision of history and continuity for identity formation, values for ideology development, a sex ethic that legitimates the normalcy of libidinal drives but inhibits their unbridled expression, a respectful and loving attitude toward middle-aged parents—Judaism can serve as a primary resource for helping the modern adolescent explore and clarify the major concerns of his or her life. Studying Judaism may not resolve all the problems, but will at least address them.

The task of educated parents and professionals is to comprehend Jewish tradition in its own language, and then translate it into a language that the adolescent can understand. The new language mediates the relationship between parent and child, professional and client, and enhances the substance of their interaction. The adolescent's intellectual curiosity may then take over in the search for meaning as a Jew.

*Chapter 5*

# COMBATING NARCISSISM
# IN THE JEWISH FAMILY

In previous chapters, a case has been made for the right of the individual to assert a difference with the prevailing authority system. This right was not deemed to be absolute, for it was limited to the realm of the intellect and did not obtain on the level of action. In modern times when choice is pluralized, and authority is not centralized, the individual has more leeway to select a personal life style. In social units such as the family where authority is vested in the institutional role of parents, the child's assertion of independence was seen as essential to normal development. However, in order to achieve healthy growth, this drive for independence had to balance the parents' need to exercise authority. The child becomes self-reliant when making choices through a relationship of interdependence.

There are times when the drive for independence and self-expression turns into narcissism. Narcissism is reflected in the degree to which the individual has difficulty maintaining a clear, differentiated sense of self and others. The narcissistic individual tends to shift from annexing another to feeling engulfed by another. It is not simply a description of self-absorption but also a tendency to lose the self in the world (Carrilio, 1981).

Though narcissism embodies these contradictory facets, this chapter will focus on self-absorption, which is a more widespread perception of the phenomenon. After discerning the impact of narcissism on the values and relationships of the family, discussion shifts to an examination of the factors that evoke narcissism, and to Judaic and professional approaches for combating it.

## THE IMPACT OF NARCISSISM ON THE FAMILY

Christopher Lasch (1978) has described our era as "the Culture of Narcissism," an outgrowth of the importance our society attaches to the individual and his or her fulfillment. "To live for the moment is the prevailing passion—to live for yourself, not for your predecessors or posterity. We are fast losing the sense of historical continuity, the sense of belonging to a succession of generations originating in the past and stretching into the future (p. 6)." A terser definition of narcissism has been offered by Marin, (cited in Reiner, 1979) as the "trend toward the deification of the isolated self (p. 5)." In the psychoanalytic literature, it is described as the individual's failure to maintain healthy object relations.

The culture of narcissism has made a deep impact on family values and relationships. More and more people are opting to shun marriage and remain single. The singles scene is a growing phenomenon. Whether the motivation stems from a fear of intimacy and giving of the self or an ideological conviction that marriage and family should not be permitted to interfere with self-development, singlehood fosters a heightened preoccupation with the self that could lead to narcissism and loneliness.

In recent times, there has been an increase in the number of couples who are living together without being formally married.    This arrangement reveals a wish for self-gratification without the responsibilities of a commitment. Such a relationship tends to be ephemeral, for each partner knows that either could terminate it at will. The couple's unwillingness to make a clear commitment to each other demonstrates their fear of intimacy and involvement, and their wish for freedom to enter into other relationships.

Marriages are threatened by dissolution due to the tendency toward narcissism. Each partner seeks gratification of personal needs from the other. Many marriages are entered into for this reason—that the spouse will fill the inner gaps. The thought is anathema that in marriage each partner should be loving and strive to make the other happy by satisfying the other's needs *first*. The concept of open marriage, where each partner is free to pursue interests and goals even as they also function as a married couple, is an apt reflection of the value of self-actualization where the satisfaction of the other's needs has traditionally been the primary goal.

Many such marriages are childless by conviction, for children are seen as interfering with the couple's drive toward self-realization. In families with children, young children are seen as pleasureless burdens and older children frequently become extensions of the need to validate one's life. Children either get in the way of parents' plans and activities, or they never really measure up to their expectations, thus fostering in parents a sense of failure in their role performance. Mothers are in conflict between their wish to be mothers, and their wish to develop themselves. This conflict takes a toll of the mother's self-image and produces tensions in her marital and family relationships.

Housewives berate themselves because they have failed to become "an amalgam of an orgastic playmate, intellectual stimulator, emotional empathizer, cathartic absorber, and autonomous strong woman (Strean, 1979, p. 43)." They not only expect much of themselves but as much, if not more, from their husbands. Husbands often feel desperate in not being a "complete sexual athlete, provider of profound wisdom and plenty of money." They fantasize that their wives could be more motherly, tender, supportive, and feminine, but concomitantly ecstatically erotic, decisive, and brilliant (p. 43). These contradictory fantasies and wishes appear to be based on primitive desires. Life is perceived to contain few limits and controls. If we cannot enjoy our job, marriage, or neighborhood, we can switch. "Similar to the young child, many adults believe that paradise and constant joy can be achieved (p. 43)." In speaking of the contemporary family, Margaret Mead (cited in Strean) has described it as consisting of "people who neglect our children, are afraid of our children, and find children a surplus instead of the *raison d'etre* of living (p. 42)." These attitudes reflect a heightened absorption with the self and with its gratification.

Narcissism appears to be a widespread phenomenon in modern society that affects all strata of the social structure, including individuals, families, and social groupings. The Jewish family is not immune from its influence.

## FACTORS CONTRIBUTING TO NARCISSISM

What are some of the sources of narcissism? What factors in the society and within the individual contribute to the deification of the self?

Berger's (1977) conceptualization of the division of social life into public and private spheres can serve as an appropriate vehicle for understanding some of the origins and dynamics of this phenomenon. The public sphere is represented by the megastructures such as the work place and bureaucracy. The private sphere is composed of the family, church, neighborhood, voluntary association, and subculture. Unable to find identity through work, the modern person turns increasingly toward the private sphere, most notably the family, for the confirmation of identity. It is as if to say: "If you really want to know who I am, come home and meet my family." But such identity seeking and finding has become quite elusive because the private sphere is underinstitutionalized. Lacking the structure and norms of the work place, the family situation creates a sense of normlessness and insecurity. This is due to the fact that family members are thrown back upon themselves to make many more decisions regarding their daily lives than heretofore. Since many families lack these capacities, the centrifugal forces of the external environment pull family members in different directions, leading to a lack of cohesion.

What Berger calls "institutionalized psychologism" (p. 32)—the proliferation of various therapies and self-improvement measures in the private sphere—supplies anxious consumers with services to construct, maintain, and repair identities. They provide the structure and meaning that is sorely lacking in family life. Narcissism is one outcome of this phenomenon. It reflects the extreme privatism and over-emphasis on the self that seem to prevail even among people who have been active in social causes. It is an exaggeration of the value of individualism which is endemic to Western society.

The turning inward also appears to be a response to emotional factors: a sense of inner emptiness, fantasies of omnipotence, and avoidance of close relationships that might release feelings of rage. Narcissism is a defense against latent depression and lack of self-esteem, a feeling of irrelevance that is one of the most pervasive emotions today (Reiner, 1979).

The loss of self-esteem and absorption with the self constitute a regression to early childhood. Freud described primary narcissism as the natural state of the infant and the source of healthy self-esteem later on in life. Adler posited that what a person needs most is to feel secure in self-esteem. When natural narcissism is combined with the basic need for self-esteem, the person has to feel oneself an object of primary value, first in the universe. The human being must stand out, be a hero, make a contribution to the world, and show that he or she counts more than anything or anyone else. Human selfishness, therefore, is an essential part of human nature. It is at the heart of the urge to cosmic heroism, according to Becker, (1973) which takes different forms such as building an edifice that reflects human value: a temple, a skyscraper, a family that spans three generations. People's hope and belief is that the things that they create in society will be of lasting worth and meaning, will outlive death and decay; that people and their products count. They must believe that their activities are timeless and meaningful.

Becker's description of the hero is akin to Soloveitchik's (1965) depiction of Adam I—the human type whose divine mandate spurs the individual to use all intellectual endowments to create a society. The aim is to become a hero whose monuments will be everlasting and will reflect upon one's greatness.

Becker's hero is also motivated to express self-worth by the fear of death. Heroism is a reflex of the terror of death. The consciousness of death impels people to quantify and control time because of its brevity. Awareness of a limited lifetime stimulates the creative gesture and is a source of anxiety over the fear of failure. But giving expression to the heroic impulse may also lead to its unbridled gratification. A person could be so driven by the fear of death and the need to actualize the self that this drive becomes unbounded and leads to hedonism and self-love. Narcissism as self-love is a distorted response to the drive for heroism. For true heroism has always been fulfilled in a social context: courage in battle, raising a family, building a synagogue, and so on. The true hero wants to make an everlasting contribution to society; the narcissist's gift is motivated by self-aggrandizement.

The issue can now be joined. For the child, narcissism is a natural tendency for the fulfillment of survival needs. In the adult, narcissism is an aberration of the drive toward heroism. It also emerges when the adult feels lonely, irrelevant, and powerless, and thereupon turns inward. Narcissism of either the heroic or the powerless type usually contains a hedonistic component.

## Combating Narcissism

Adult narcissism appears to be a deep-seated phenomenon that is a function of the individual's early biography and the impact of sociocultural processes. It is a pervasive feature of the modern human condition and as such, difficult to change. Yet an attempt must be made to confront the issue and to hold out the possibility that the individual can overcome the tendency to self-absorption, and learn how to reach out to others.

### JUDAIC APPROACHES

Two Judaic approaches for combating narcissism will now be explored, to be followed by professional approaches: 1) the need to control hedonistic impulses and recognize one's limitations as a creative being, i.e., self-renunciation; and 2) the need to reach out to others without losing oneself in the process, i.e., the capacity for self-transcendence. The first, represented by the thought of Joseph B. Soloveitchik, reflects a preoccupation with the self, the existential crisis; the second, explicated by David Hartman, reflects a preoccupation with the other person, the wholeness of relationship.

### The Self-Renunciation Approach

Loneliness is a pervasive theme in Soloveitchik's philosophical thought (1965) An existential phenomenon, it contrasts with aloneness which is a social category. One's aloneness motivates one to join with others in order to produce a society. Thus, maintaining social contacts and working together with others serve utilitarian purposes. Such social relationships are functionally oriented, designed to enhance the self-esteem of the individual through productive acts. Human creativity is a fulfillment of God's mandate "to fill the earth and subdue it (Gen. 1:28)." It is an act of originality and self-assertion, an externalization of the self into the world.

Existential loneliness is a state of being. The lonely individual does not strive for the externalization of the self into the world, but for the internalization of the world into the self. There is a passive quality to the lonely individual's relation to the world. One's goal in life is to be redeemed, a process that requires withdrawal. Redemption comes when one admits helplessness and surrenders one's self to God. There are times when one experiences intimacy with God, and there are times when God seems distant and unattainable. It is when God seems unreachable that loneliness becomes overwhelming.

Soloveitchik maintains that, in spite of the loneliness of the single self, communication and community are still possible; in spite of being lonely, one can experience the loving response of another. A redeemed existence is ultimately a communal form of existence; "the individual and the communal religious norm are inextricably bound together...the inner spiritual life of the individual finds expression in the shared experiences of community (Hartman, 1978, p. 216)." In his oral and literary works, Soloveitchik (1978) has developed various conceptions of community. The notion of community is not inconsequential to his philosophic thought. It seems, however, that he lays greater stress—both intellectually and emotionally—on explicating the phenomenon of existential loneliness, on the individual's relation to God and the world, and on one's goals in life. Since man was created a lonely being (Sanhedrin, 37a), the single human being occupies a more prominent place than the community in Soloveitchik's anthropology. I have, therefore, opted to focus on this component of his thought in order to develop an approach for combating narcissism. It has been said that people strive for heroism, for leaving an everlasting monument to their existence after they are gone. The heroic drive is expressed through creative actions which, when aimed at self-gratification, can lead to narcissism. The person who engages in creative work finds it difficult to renounce the world and the self. Such renunciation contradicts the drive for the heroic, for making an indelible impression on the world. Yet it is a necessary prerequisite for achieving redemption.

The question is, how can man be creative and achieve redemption simultaneously? Both Becker and Soloveitchik grappled with this question. In Becker's (1973) words:

> The real problem of genius: how to develop a creative work with the full force of one's passion, a work that saves one's soul, and at the same time to renounce that very work because it cannot by itself give salvation (p. 173).

The creative work saves one's soul because it represents the ultimate in the individual's externalization of the self; the deepest expression of the personality is imprinted upon the canvas, the book, the ideology, the architecture. Yet it cannot give salvation because once externalized, it becomes an object independent of the person, resulting in a vacuum within the self. Salvation seems to require an ongoing relationship, not a separation between the self and the object of its creation. For Becker, religion is the only means for resolving this paradox of the human situation. Religion enables the person to expand as an heroic personality and to surrender one's existence to a higher being. It takes human creatureliness and insignificance, and makes them a condition of hope. The full transcendence of the human condition through belief in God means limitless possibilities for the individual's activities as a creative being (p. 204).

Soloveitchik (1978) has enunciated a similar idea as the essence of the Jew's religious experience. He asks, "What is heroism in the *Halakhah*? . . . The answer is: one must perform the dialectical movement." This means to drive forward toward conquest and victory, and when they are within reach, to stop short, turn around, and retreat. At the most exalted moment of triumph, one must forego the ecstasy of victory and take defeat at one's own hands. This dialectical movement applies to all aspects of human experience—the aesthetic, the emotional, the intellectual, and the moral-religious. "In a word, the *Halakhah* teaches man how to conquer and how to lose, how to seize initiative and how to renounce, how to succeed, how to invite defeat, and how to resume the striving for victory (p. 44)."

How does the *Halakhah* do this? By offering a model of behavior through the *mitzvot* that encourages the Jew to expand horizons, tap the earth's natural resources, and build a society. But the freedom that is the person's to create and to build is granted within limitations. Two notable examples are: the Sabbath day of rest after a 6-day work week, which requires withdrawal from the pursuit of heroism and acknowledgement of one's limitations as a creative being; and the abstinence from conjugal relations during the wife's menstrual cycle and 7 days thereafter—the *niddah* period—when the couple must withdraw from physical contact (pp. 45-46).

Emotional life must also be controlled. Laws such as "thou shalt not covet" (Ex. 20:14) and "thou shalt not hate thy brother in thy heart" (Lev. 19:17) are as integral a part of the Judaic normative system as are those related to action. A classic example which effectively conveys this idea is the cessation of *avelut*—mourning practices—at the onset of a Jewish holiday. If a person suffers the loss of a close relative *erev ha-chag*—on the day before the holiday—the *Halakhah* requires the bereaved to sit *shiva* —observe mourning rituals—if only for an hour, then change into holiday clothing and prepare to enter the holiday in a spirit of joy and festivity. What happens to the grief? How does one express it? It is apparent, concludes Soloveitchik, that the *Halakhah* believed people capable of controlling their emotions for the sake of a transcendent value—the communal celebration of an historical event. Not only *must* they suppress their grief, but they *can!* Since people may not mourn during public celebrations, they will have to come to terms with their grief in their own way. The Torah believes the person to be master over one's inner world.

Thus, Soloveitchik posits the act of withdrawal expressed through self-restraint and the surrender to a higher power as the means for achieving redemption. Ontological meaning does not derive from acts of conquest but from their renunciation. The *Halakhah* helps one to achieve a balance between these conflicting tendencies. To receive the divine norm requires surrender of the will, but to actualize it requires the creative act. Self-assertion needs to be followed by withdrawal, which is always temporary, for the individual is called upon once again to advance. The halakhic individual successfully oscillates between these two modes of being. The non-halakhic individual does not, because withdrawal represents defeat, which is an intolerable affront to one's self-image as a hero.

In sum, unbridled heroism leads to excessive absorption and expansion of the self which results in self-deification or narcissism. In order to counter this tendency, one needs to balance the heroic impulse with gestures of renunciation, to feel and believe that the creative act alone does not provide the answer to the search for meaning. It is only through realization of mortality and finiteness that a balance can be achieved. To Soloveitchik, the halakhic tradition helps one to surrender the self through acts of self-restraint. It is this characteristic of Judaism that Soloveitchik emphasizes in his quest for understanding the loneliness of the faith experience and the essential nature of the human being.

Narcissism, from this perspective, can be combated by the modern Jewish family through entry into the stream of the halakhic tradition. A particular mental set is then created—that all forward movement in productive work, intellectual understanding, social relationships, and creative activity needs to be tempered by withdrawal. This approach requires a consciousness of finiteness, an awareness that the self is limited in what it can externalize, and that existential loneliness and powerlessness can be overcome by attachment to a higher being. It appeals to the individual's urge for the faith experience. The self-renunciation approach introduces a religious atmosphere into the home, as belief in God and surrender to His will check tendencies toward self-absorption and personal gratification. Family members reach out to each other as they reach out to God in the process of forming a faith community.

The self-renunciation approach is neither accessible nor enticing to the majority of Jewish families, for it presupposes a deeply religious attitude which is alien to them. It is conceivable that Jewish families for whom the halakhic tradition is central to their world outlook would not be afflicted by narcissistic tendencies. It is also possible that they may, due to the influences of contemporary values. If there exists no ideological conflict between the halakhic call for self-surrender and society's encouragement of narcissistic pursuits because Jewish values are limited to ritual performance and are not applied to the struggles of daily living, there is little hope for change. If, however, these families should experience an ideological conflict because for them Jewish and societal values clash over the definition of the human being's function in the world, there is a chance for narcissism to be overcome through the confrontation.

## The Self-Transcendence Approach

A second Judaic approach to combat narcissism can be discerned in the writings of David Hartman and the publications of the Shalom Hartman Institute. This approach is relational rather than existential, social as opposed to individual. It asserts that one gains fulfillment primarily in social contexts, and when one reaches out to others one creates oneself.

Thus an alternate way to combat narcissism is to enter into social relationships which require mutual dependency and empathy. Every meaningful relationship requires interdependence, as each partner gives and cares for the other. Mature object relations presuppose self-love that can be transcended in the person of the other.

This is not merely a modern humanistic approach but an essential feature of Jewish consciousness and values. This consciousness is not individualistic, lonely, and defeated, but intersubjective, relational and interdependent. Hartman does not deny the self-control, withdrawal component, for it is a cornerstone of the halakhic system; however, he chooses to emphasize the *Halakhah's* interpersonal element because it is the essential characteristic of God's covenantal relationship with Israel. In an address to American Jewish community leaders, Hartman (1978) dealt with the theme of interdependence which is the essence of *tzedakah*— the social welfare institution in Judaism.

> In the Jewish tradition, to be human is not to be embarrassed by your dependence on others. When the Bible says, "It is not good for man to be alone" (Gen. 2:18), what it is claiming is that man becomes fully human only in the context of interdependence. To love another human being is to abandon the ideal of self-sufficiency and absolute independence; to love is to be able to say, "I need you." One who is frightened of needing someone else cannot experience the depths of love. God in the Bible loves man because God, as it were, deeply needs man (p. 32).

Hartman perceives in the laws of *tzedakah* the opportunity for each Jew to deal with people in need and to help them develop the capacity to love. If the giver responds manipulatively to their needs, they will become embarrassed to expose their needs to another human being. But by being gentle and supportive of someone's helplessness, the giver enables the helped to discover that there is no shame to being human, i.e., to be in need of others. The highest form of helping, of giving *tzedakah,* according to Maimonides (1956, Laws of Gifts to the Poor, X, 7) is to help a person become self-supporting and not be humiliated by poverty. Maimonides continues:

> If a poor man requests money from you and you have nothing to give him, speak to him consolingly. It is forbidden to upbraid a poor person or to shout at him because his heart is broken and contrite...Woe to him who shames a poor man (X, 5).

Maimonides is sensitive to a problem that many people, particularly doctors and helping professionals, face. How do we respond to people whom we cannot help? How do we react to people when our inability to satisfy their needs exposes our inadequacies? "The ability to respond to another," Hartman (1978) concludes, "even though this response will not solve the other's problems completely, is an important feature of mature interdependency (p. 47)."

While the obligation to respond to another is incumbent on the Jew at all times, it is particularly emphasized during times of celebration. At Passover every family is urged to invite those who are hungry to share in the Seder. During the Purim festivities each Jew is required to reach out to the poor to enable them to share in the communal joy. Maimonides (Laws of Holidays) describes the goal of celebrating the holiday in a spirit of *simha*—joy.

> And men should eat meat and drink wine, for there can be no real rejoicing without meat and wine to drink. And while one eats and drinks himself, it is his duty to feed the stranger, the orphan, the widow, and other poor and un-

fortunate people, for he who locks the doors to his courtyard and eats and drinks with his wife and family, without
giving anything to eat and drink to the poor and the bitter
in soul—his meal is not a rejoicing in a divine commandment, but a rejoicing in his own stomach (VI, 18).

The *mitzvah* of *simha* is associated with the joy that derives from
good food and drink, and not from the experience of joy which
is self-indulgent and narcissistic. "Judaism rejects the joy of
physical gratification when it is egocentric and expressive of
one's indifference to the joy of others (Purim, 1981)." When I
include others in my experience as an obligation of sharing,
this act represents the core experience of the joy of life.

> Joy and responsibility are not antithetical pos-
> tures. . . *Mitzvah* and *simcha* are not incompatible but,
> rather, coincide to the extent that both undermine the
> barriers separating the self from the other. A test of whe-
> ther one has fulfilled the halakhic norm of *simha* is whether
> one has felt the outer-directed feelings of love and em-
> pathy for others.

> On Purim we make contact with the child's unself-
> conscious joy of life. And in making contact with this
> child-like joy of life, we discover a new dimension of the
> adult world of *mitzvah;* we discover sensitivity to the needs
> of others born of the celebration of life (p. 6).

This concept of Purim and the concomitant obligation to share
one's joy with others reflect the *Halakhah's* attempt to address
the problem of self-centeredness and the loss of a sense of
transcendence.

Complementing the halakhic approach, the Midrash offers an insight into the dynamics of personality development
that addresses this theme. The Midrash states that the *yetzer
hara*—evil impulse—enters the individual at birth and the *yetzer
hatov*—good impulse—at the age of thirteen years. (The Fathers According to Rabbi Nathan, 16). For girls it's at age
twelve. The evil impulse can be defined as "the principle of
self-imprisonment." The person it pervades needs to be in con-

trol of the environment. Such an individual cannot genuinely love since love presupposes acceptance of the other's independence. One withdraws from relationships which one cannot fully control. One cannot respond to any ethical "ought" since one is not predisposed to accept ethical claims which override self-interest.

The problem facing the rabbis was not simply that of teaching what Torah requires of people, but also of rehabilitating the character structure of the self-encapsulated individual. They struggled against the development and expression of those human character traits which seal a person off from another person, from community, from ethical claims, and from God (Evil Impulse, 1981).

The principle of relationship characterizes the covenant between Israel and God which was concluded at Sinai. The tradition of *mitzvot* may be viewed as a framework through which one may transcend self-centeredness into a relational context with the divine Other. The tradition, therefore, taught that the *yetzer hatov*—the good impulse—begins to operate in a boy when he reaches thirteen, the age of moral and legal accountability. Only as one begins to move beyond the narcissism of childhood, represented by the *yetzer hara,* does one become receptive to the commanding voice of *mitzvah.*

The *Halakhah* viewed the social structure of the family as developing in its members the capacity to accept interdependence without feeling that dependence on others is a regression to infancy. "One of the main functions of the family in Judaism is to counteract the myth of radical individualism and self-sufficiency (p. 5)." Family members need each other in order to survive as a group. Judaism has built into the interpersonal relationships of the family values and obligations regarding love, honor, reverence, service, giving and receiving.

In many Jewish families today, this relational system is apparently not working. Family members are pulling away from each other and moving into themselves. The self-transcendence approach can appeal to the modern Jewish family. It does not demand a faith commitment but is concerned with the relational dimension of everyday life. Thus it has a universal component, though its value base is steeped in the religious tradition. The relational approach invites the narcissist to become involved with others, to step out of a self-centered world to give of oneself and to lean on others. Such sharing and dependency enable one to become more human and whole. In contrast to the self-renunciation approach which is a contraction of the self and reserved for the few, the self-transcendence approach is an expansion of the self and accessible to the many.

## PROFESSIONAL APPROACHES

The phenomenon of narcissism is difficult to deal with professionally because it is embedded in the pervasive value orientations of modern society. It affects individuals not only as private citizens, but in their public lives as professionals. The professional is a product of a society where competitive individualism has as its goal the pursuit of happiness, which could result in a preoccupation with the self. The professional may or may not become narcissistic, but is not above the influence of the individualistic orientation.

The professional brings the individualistic orientation into his or her work not only from exposure to societal values, but also to professional education. Education for the helping professions, particularly the therapeutic enterprise, tends to foster an emphasis on the individual. When therapists speak of the need for meaning and love, they define them simply as the fulfillment of the client's emotional requirements. They do not encourage the client to subordinate his or her interests to others, or to a cause or tradition outside the self. The client often becomes the narrow focus of the therapist's lens. The therapist may encourage and support goals of self-expression, self-awareness, self-fulfillment and even self-preoccupation at the expense of family stability. The values clustered around the self may become the goals of individually-oriented psychotherapy.

Despite the therapeutic thrust toward developing the individual's self-reliance, many individuals cannot shoulder the consequences of their own decisions for they do not possess the wisdom, maturity, and life experience to do so. This is particularly true of adolescents and young adults who become immobilized at a time when their need to be independent prevents them from seeking their parents' advice. Under these conditions their individualism becomes exaggerated, and their self-absorption severs the universe of discourse that had once obtained in the family. The young people who attempt to make it on their own do meet with a modicum of success, but with failure and frustration along the way.

The resolution of the problem lies in a reorientation to the concept of family in the therapeutic experience. Various approaches in family therapy, along with family systems theory, place the family in the center of the therapeutic effort. They proclaim the notion that "the family group is central to the development and well-being of its members, and that this family unit has within it powerful resources for the promotion of healthy change (Lang, 1980, p. 303)." The *family* becomes the client; *it* is the unit of service, rather than the individuals who comprise it. The understanding of clients' difficulties through a family-oriented approach is central to shaping agency services and professional training. When fully understood and accepted, it organizes the professional's response toward a true pro-family stance.

The difference between an individualistic stance and a family approach can be discerned in a typical divorce case. A frantic woman calls the agency or the therapist for an appointment to discuss the pending breakup of her marriage. She wants to be seen alone. The individually-oriented therapist would be inclined to respond to her need, and explore her conflicts, anxieties, etc., without connecting them to the family complex. This focus on the individual client causes the therapist to view her dilemma exclusively from her perspective. The family therapist would insist that both spouses be seen and would work through any resistance to this approach. He or she may call in the children and other relatives at various points in the treatment process. This orientation communicates to the client that divorce is not a private affair, that marital conflict is two-sided, and the implications for the spouses and the children—the family as a whole—are too wide-reaching and consequential for undimensional therapy.

Lang summarizes this approach convincingly:

> The therapist who views the family unit as "client" makes a powerful *value* statement which acts as a counterbalance to the American cultural value of individualistic goals. Divorce is a family affair, and seeing the family as a natural group underlines respect for the family, for "its still beating heart," and implies recognition that divorce will have a continuing impact on all family members. A family approach frequently mobilizes family members to reexamine troubled relationships together, and may tap unexpected reserves of strength in this process. Individual issues of self-fulfillment are not discounted, but are blended into the family gestalt and understood in that context (p. 303).

The family approach is not only useful in divorce situations, but also in intergenerational relationships. In a conflict between aged parents and adult children, the family therapist views intergenerational loyalties and dependency as natural components in such relationships and would insist that they deal with the issues and the feelings in face to face encounters. The family approach makes respectable the notions of responsibility, loyalty, obligation, and even self-sacrifice (p. 304).

*Summary and Conclusions*

This chapter has focused on one of the more prominent variables of narcissism, the absorption with the self. Narcissism is seen to be a complex phenomenon, with origins in the social structure, cultural values, and the individual's psychological upbringing. In an achievement-oriented society, striving to be a hero can become such a consuming drive that the individual loses perspective on the tenuousness of his or her creations. The fear of failure is an impelling motive to succeed, with little or no regard for the constraints due to one's mortality. Unbridled zealousness for success is accompanied by feelings of loneliness, and fantasies of omnipotence accentuate the lack of self-esteem. Both contribute to the individual's absorption with the self and the inability and fear in becoming involved with others.

The social toll of narcissism is widespread. Family relationships are more tenuous, as marriage partners expect each other to fulfill unrealistic demands; parents and children function on different wave lengths, with each absorbed in a separate world. Singlehood is a preferred value to marriage, and marriage is valued without parenthood.

Both Judaic and professional approaches to combating narcissism have been described. The ''self-renunciation'' approach, derived from my understanding of the philosophy of Soloveitchik, offers Jewish families an opportunity to become immersed in the search for faith and belief in the transcendent all-powerful God in whose presence all human effort pales. In this conception of the human relationship with God, the family surrenders its selfhood, and becomes consumed with doing His will. It bends its will and is no longer driven solely by the heroic impulse. The obedient personality is not narcissistic but ''altruistic.'' One is not absorbed with oneself, but with the other. The self is contracted upon entering a relationship of dependency with God.

This approach is reserved for the few in the Jewish community who are able to renounce selfhood in the face of an achievement-oriented society. For them the experience of faith is lonely. It is a difficult life style to maintain and perpetuate. The "self-transcendence" approach, postulated by Hartman, does not require renunciation of the self, but its full expression through involvement with the other. Its thrust is relational, for it believes that human fulfillment is conditional upon the ability to enter into relationships with others. In this process, the individual family members first seek to transcend themselves in the family unit; they develop an identification with the family as a whole, which provides the umbrella for their self-definition. As a paradigm for all social relationships, the family enables its members to embrace other social situations with natural feelings of interdependence.

In Jewish tradition the theological source for this approach is the covenant between God and Israel, and the pragmatic source is in the values and laws of *tzedakah*. Both require the individual to enter into a relationship that bespeaks obligation and responsibility. The self, in this approach, is not denied but enhanced, for it expands to include the other.

Professional approaches to combat narcissism encourage therapists and others working with families to reorient their thinking from an individualistic to a family concept. The cognitive, perceptual shift must be based on a fundamental change in the professional's value system. The issue, however, is not either/or, with either the individual or the family valued. Both are valued for their own sake, for it is believed that the individual cannot develop fully without dynamic interaction with the family. Efforts to do so in isolation are doomed to failure.

The professional working with troubled families will need to have knowledge of the social causes of dysfunction including systems theory, in order to view the individual's problem within the social context of the whole family. If the family is the original locus of the problem, therein lies its resolution. Narcissistic tendencies that create centrifugal forces in the family can be overcome through a therapeutic process in which family members confront their commitments, responsibilities, and feelings toward each other. Therapy will have been effective if the family as a whole is deemed more important than the sum of its parts, if each individual is transcended by the group.

When professionals begin to shift their perception of the individual as the value, to include the family as the value, they will have broadened their scope of the etiology of the problem. This presupposes that they will have become more conscious of the impact of societal values on their own consciousness and behavior. Self-awareness enables the professional to control the input into the helping process, so that the client's needs will be served more objectively. If he or she values the family, the professional will seek the appropriate opportunities to involve the family in the problems of its members. Then the client will no longer feel alone, will not be permitted to become self-absorbed, but will be encouraged to work the problem through in the context of the family.

*Chapter 6*

# THE FAITH AND PATHOLOGY OF HOLOCAUST SURVIVOR FAMILIES

Previous chapters which have dealt with authority and autonomy, the independence of children, models of Jewish family life in the authority-independence context, adolescence, and approaches toward combating narcissism have addressed the Jewish family in general. Now a particular type of Jewish family will be studied where the authority-autonomy conflict permeates the parent-child relationship in pathological ways, owing to the devastating impact of a terrible experience on their lives. The holocaust's impact on survivors and their children has been profound and extensive. While I cannot hope to encompass all its facets, an attempt will be made to better understand the faith and pathology of survivor families from the perspective of the professional's functions.

The subject of holocaust survivors and their children has always evoked feelings of unease and discomfort in me, despite having written about it (Linzer, 1978) and taught it for many years at the Wurzweiler School of Social Work. My difficulty in approaching the subject stems from several sources: 1) the impossible task of placing oneself as a helping professional in the person of the survivor, struggling to imagine what occurred, and the nature of the experiences lived through. I believe they are beyond the realm of even the most empathic and insightful professional. 2) I feel humble in the presence of people who displayed superhuman strength in affirming the human vitality for life, and for bringing children into the world, despite experiences of *hurban*—destruction, terror, and dehumanization. This emotional response sometimes interferes with my ability to perceive clearly and objectively the issues involved in teaching about survivors and their children. 3) I feel overwhelmed by our responsibility as educators and helping professionals to stop the generational effects of the holocaust from penetrating the grandchildren's lives, and where it already has, to stifle its growth there. Hence the need to think through, to feel, to share ideas, to clarify issues.

## Definition

At the outset, it is necessary to define the survivor and the survivor's children. The significance of this task was highlighted for me at a seminar with the professional staff of a Jewish family agency, conducted by the late Dr. Esther Appelberg of the Wurzweiler School under the auspices of the Jewish Orientation and Training Seminar of the Board of Jewish Education of Greater New York. She asked the question, "Who is a survivor?" There was a stunned silence. All participants seemed to think that the definition was obvious. During the discussion, when several realized that they, too, could be considered survivors, a vivid emotional response was visible on their faces.

Who is a survivor? Kestenberg (1972) asserts that it is easier to define the children of survivors than the survivors themselves. Survivors' children are those who were born after the holocaust or had been removed from the centers of persecution before they suffered from it directly, and were later reunited with one or both surviving parents. As for survivors, there is general agreement that they include those who were liberated from the concentration camps, were persecuted by the Nazis, or hid and escaped from Nazi surveillance. There is some doubt whether to include Jews who fled European countries immediately prior to the Nazi invasion.

## RELIGIOUS ASPECTS: FAITH AND RITUAL

In this context, religious aspects refers to the theological question regarding God's presence in the holocaust, and the depth of the holocaust's impact on the Jewish identity, faith, and ritual observance of the survivor.

The universal need for theodicy as an explanation of evil is well-known. The need emerges on the communal and individual levels. The community must explain such mass catastrophes as war, revolution, drought, and earthquakes in the life of the group; the individual seeks reasons for death, illness, loss, and poverty in the life of the family. Theodicy is the religious legitimation of anomic phenomena (Berger, 1968).

In a society where many gods are responsible for different functions, the presence of evil can be ascribed to one in particular, e.g., Zoroastrianism. In Jewish society, where monotheism is the dominant ideology, ascribing evil to a God who is deemed good becomes problematic. During World War II in most of the countries of Europe, Jews felt abandoned by their God. They could not understand what happened to the promises God made to them through Abraham, at Sinai, to the prophets. If, indeed, they were chosen, a "peculiar treasure," a holy nation, why were they, a people who are God's children, decimated? They felt forsaken by God, and their faith and commitment to the covenant was shaken (Kolitz, 1968).

Jewish theologians have struggled in vain to discover a rationale, an explanation that would make the horror plausible. Buber (1952) offered the notion of *hester panim*, the "eclipse of God." God's withdrawal from history is the cause of havoc, turmoil, and ravage in human affairs. Schachter (1968) offered the sinfulness of the Jews as the cause for their suffering. Rubinstein (1966) proclaimed that the God of history was dead. Wiesel actually saw him hanging on the gallows (1960) but then wondered how one cannot believe in him after what had happened (1969). Some attempted to discover the divine plan that connected the establishment of the State of Israel with the holocaust (1967). All of the aforementioned explanations or theories have been deemed unacceptable for they do not lend meaning to the struggles of the deceased and the survivors, and to the enormity of the event. A theology of Auschwitz may never be developed.

On the personal level, holocaust survivors have asked the "why?" question of the deaths of family members, of the misery they feel in their lives such as nightmares of persecution, mistrust of others, insecurity, and other emotional and mental disturbances. They feel themselves to be damaged people, damaged forever because they are Jews who are an eternally persecuted people (Appleberg, 1972).

While we know that holocaust survivors have strong feelings about their traumatic experiences as Jews, until the recent book by Brenner (1980) there had been a paucity of empirical research on their faith and Jewish identity. Research has primarily focused on their psychopathologic symptoms and behavior. In an older study of 100 survivors, Tuteur (1966) found that most Jewish families adhered to their faith, observed kashruth and other rituals, and did not intermarry. "I suffered because I was a Jew, I was saved by a miracle, I am not able to give up my belief even if I do not understand the reason for my persecution," is a statement heard from many respondents. The author unqualifiedly asserts that religious belief was unshaken despite the inhuman treatment and ubiquitous fear of death. Yet, this type of response was not universal. The following story indicates the anger that still persists after so many years. A religious woman who is observant in all ways, always places a drop of milk in her chicken soup and says, "This is to punish you, God, for what you have done." Another survivor relates this story of his disaffection for a Jewish ritual.

I was in the Lodz ghetto and knew Rombowski the head of the ghetto, not well, but to say hello to. He cared very much for all the children. One day I went out to look for food. My little sister was hungry and cried for something to eat. But there was nothing at all to be had. I ran from place to place looking everywhere, anywhere there had been some food to be had previously. Nothing at all. I returned home empty-handed.

I walked slowly, afraid to rush back empty-handed, thinking how could I tell my sister that I could bring her nothing to eat. I didn't know what I'd say but it turned out I didn't have to explain a thing to my little sister. She was gone when I arrived. They had come for her and taken her away while I was gone. I too would have been taken to my death then had she not saved my life by sending me on the fruitless task of trying to locate something to eat for her all over the ghetto. That errand kept me alive, but I never saw her alive.

It's been 25 years or more since then but no day passes by without my thinking about that day, without my thinking about the room's emptiness, my sister's little belongings on the floor, a doll, a torn sweater, one window a trifle open with the curtain drawn and sucked outside by the draft, the table empty of food, a book from which I had been reading to her opened to the page I was up to and was to continue to read to her after I returned with something to eat.

And my tephillin. I could never bring myself to wear tephillin again. The blue velvet bag was there on the table and I have a picture in my mind of my sister, before being

> taken away, touching it once, quickly kissing it, as she had done piously, religiously, lovingly, with me in the room watching approvingly as though kissing it was itself a religious act and at the same time, since it was my talit and tephillin which she saw me—her older brother whom she loved and who protected her—wear at prayers, it was as though she was kissing me when she was bringing it to her lips devotedly. I cannot look at tephillin without remembering that scene, without tears and without despair. I simply cannot look at another pair of tephillin (Brenner, pp. 52–53).

Can we conclude from these heart-rending stories that these survivors' anger and bitterness render them irreligious, that the *hutzpah*—defiance of the woman and the boldness of the man are anathema to a faith consciousness and religious loyalty? I think not. Their rebelliousness is in the tradition of Abraham who questioned God's justice in His intention to destroy Sodom and Gomorrah. The practice of challenging God has since been internalized in Jewish consciousness and came to full expression by holocaust survivors.

In the first story, the pious woman deliberately makes the soup *traife*—unkosher. It is an act of spite, of retribution for her suffering, but it is the act of a religious woman.

In the second story, the pious man commits an act of omission; he refrains from performing this ritual; but he gave up no other Jewish practice. The discontinuance of one *mitzvah* was apparently sufficient to proclaim his bitter resentment of God; this, too, is the act of a religious Jew.

The paradox that believing Jews can deny God but remain believers is expressed very eloquently by a survivor who worked in the clearance detail of the gas chamber, washing down the corpses with a water hose:

> You've got to be very close to God, you have to know Him very well to blaspheme Him. Only a deeply religious person can despise God, shake his fist at God and abuse Him. A blaspheming Jew is a believing Jew...Being an atheist in the camp was no easy thing (p. 100).

Many Jews believed that they were expressing their atheism by shouting God's nonexistence to His face when, in reality, they were experiencing radical abandonment. There were many shades of faith and doubt lost, reclaimed, or confirmed. This was equally true of ritual observance. One of the major variables affecting faith and practice was the depth of faith and commitment to ritual prior to the holocaust. An observant survivor was more likely to be influenced by the holocaust than his nonobservant counterpart.

A survivor who was a student at the Wurzweiler School of Social Work, laments the fact that her friends, who have by now all perished, were incarcerated in the camps even though they were assimilated Jews who didn't care about being Jewish.

> Nonetheless, the only reason for their ignominious murder is the fact that they were Jewish. And soon, they will not even be remembered as Jews; somehow I feel I contribute to their total disappearance when I think of my son, who lives in Kentucky with his lovely wife, a Southern Baptist. In all probability, their children will be raised as Baptists—whatever that is. Last year, this did not bother me. Why does it bother me now? I feel a traitor to my childhood friends a *second time:* for having escaped, and for having future grandchildren who will not be Jewish.

> The pain is all the more strange that thirty years ago, it is exactly what I would have welcomed. As a matter of fact, not having Jewish grandchildren is the result of the education I gave my children. The only way to survive, I thought, is to change one's name and hide one's origins. This was the safest protection if you valued life. I intended to protect my children at all costs. What I had endured, I would make sure they would never have to face.

> My children are safe today—and content. But it does not work for me. I don't know what happened. It is probably the fault of this course. I feel more guilty than ever towards a beloved Orthodox grandmother who died in the train en route to a camp, and towards my cherished childhood friends—all Jews in spite of themselves.

This woman thought that she could escape her Jewishness, as she was able to escape persecution. Her denial worked for many years. It enabled her to accept her son's intermarriage and her guilt-less past. But now, as she approaches old age and as she engaged in the meaning of the holocaust in the *Jewish Social Philosophy* course at the Wurzweiler School, she is pointedly reminded that she is Jewish. In reviewing her life during and after the holocaust, she experiences emotional turmoil and an identity crisis. Her self-image is shaken as she confronts herself and her life in a new perspective.

## HOLOCAUST SURVIVORS IN ISRAEL

Research conducted on survivors who emigrated to Israel after the war indicated a reduction of the psychopathologic and psychosomatic symptoms that generally afflicted survivors in other countries. When they arrived, the War of Independence was raging. Each person who fought or aided in the war effort was valued. Participation in the war fashioned a changed self-image; henceforth Jews would not go to their deaths as sheep to slaughter, but they were capable of fighting for their freedom and self-respect. Everyone contributed to the upbuilding of the land. There was a feeling of security in belonging to the Jewish nation in its own land. Thus, Hitler's grand design was thwarted in the creation of the new state (Newman, 1979).

Winnik (1967) adds that the large size of the group of survivors who had shared similar traumatic experiences helped to reduce the sense of estrangement and exclusion. Survivors were not set apart from the rest of the population because adaptation was a general problem of the new state and not a specific problem of the survivors. A craving for dependency was not encouraged, thus activating the mental powers and promoting collaboration.

Nevertheless, even within the supportive Israeli environment, psychological differences were noticeable between children of survivors and their peers. Hillel Klein (cited in

Newman, 1979) tested children on several kibbutzim and found them to have unconscious denial of conflict situations with parents and teachers, to become anxious at even short-term separations from parents, to collude with parents to deny the latter's suffering and emphasize only their heroism. As late as 1979, Davidson (1980) was describing his treatment of psychiatric disturbances in children of survivors in Israel, who appeared to reflect similar patterns to their counterparts in the United States. Thus, for many survivors, living in Israel could not eradicate the deep scars and persistent trauma that they inevitably passed down to their children.

It is interesting to note that many, if not most, of the survivors had refused to reside in kibbutzim upon arrival in Israel, despite the economic and social security which they offered. It was explained that their reluctance to lead a collective life was reminiscent of the period they were interned in the camps, and of their yearning for privacy. The kibbutzim, with their self-contained community and enclosures, reminded them of the concentration camps (Winnik, 1967).

Not all Jewish survivors made a pathological adjustment after the war, nor did they all rear traumatized children. Perhaps an important factor was their belief in Judaism and its rituals. This provided structure and continuity with history and community which was so lacking in the camps. Another factor was the identification with an ideology, provided by the fledgling Jewish state, of heroism, construction, belonging, and human worth.

In sum, the faith-ritual dimension is a fertile area for professional concern and research. Aside from Brenner's work, the literature has avoided it thus far, and has, instead, concentrated on the pathology and its treatment. But we know that a person's beliefs and values exert an important influence on self-image and behavior. Beliefs and values, Jewish identity and rituals have to be investigated if we are to gain a more comprehensive picture of the internal dynamics of survivor families. One of the professional's goals in this area of inquiry is to help them establish and maintain a viable Jewish life within the Jewish community to provide healing, uplifting of spirit, and belonging to the group.

## PROFESSIONAL ASPECTS: DEALING WITH PATHOLOGY

An extensive literature has appeared over the years concerning the professional aspects of diagnosing and treating survivors. Neiderland (1977) was among the first psychiatrists in the United States to have revealed the existence of psychiatric disturbances among survivors. Krystal's book, *Massive Psychic Trauma* (1968), has been the major work devoted to the psychiatric problems of this population. In the past 10 years, a sizable literature has emerged on the generational disturbances in survivors' children. This section will focus on the pathology of the children, and the functions, approaches, and sensitivity of the professional.

Children who are now young adults manifest exaggerated symptoms of the normal tensions faced by children in the process of separating from their parents. The problem of separation—individuation in holocaust survivor children highlighted by Freyberg (1980), can be said to have originated during the circumstances under which the parents married. Marriages which took place in the Displaced Persons camps were consummated quickly, with no prior courtship. The couple did not really know each other and each had sustained loss of family and friends. Each was extremely lonely and lacked the capacity for human emotion and love. Marriage was seen as a vehicle for overcoming loneliness and for bearing children to replace those who had perished. Having a child expressed "an almost holy commitment that the Jewish people must continue (Schiff, 1980)." It mattered little whether mates were suited to each other. There was a driving need to fill voids—physical, emotional, existential—at any cost.

Children born under these conditions soon experienced their parents' disturbances. The syndrome included inability to love and care, overprotectiveness bordering on tenacity, and inability to permit independent functioning. For young adults these problems were exacerbated. Their need to separate and become individuals on their own was thwarted, lest they be "lost" to their parents. Since children were seen as replacements for the dead, parents could not loosen their controls over their lives lest something terrible happen to them. Children who rebelled against parents were made to feel terrible guilt and shame, and when they internalized their anger it inevitably led to depression.

In many cases, the substitute for parental love was material overindulgence, which never satisfied the child's craving for emotional closeness. Children developed ambivalent attitudes towards their parents, particularly mothers.

> Case: A sixteen-year-old girl complained that "My mother is weak, she's almost dead, she didn't live after the war, and she does everything in her power for me not to live . . . but I am the only thing left in her life (Davidson, 1980)."

Parents demanded excellence and success in all their children's endeavors. Children felt tremendous pressure to succeed and not disappoint them. This fostered guilt in the children if they did not measure up to expectations.

> Case: I have the same drive. It would be more punishing for me to give up the drive to excel, to learn as much as I can . . .
> (Linzer, 1978).

Young adults, particularly, experienced great difficulty in initiating and maintaining social relationships. They discovered that they had been influenced by their parents' mistrust of other people and their suspiciousness of opening themselves to others lest a dire catastrophe ensue. They have internalized this pattern, thus complicating and retarding their capacity for intimacy and marriage.

Children tend to feel a lack of self-identity. They are unsure of who they are because, in many instances, they represent or were named after dead relatives.

> Case: My mother always tells me how beautiful I am, but I know it's not true. She's referring to my sister who was really beautiful but was killed in the war (Davidson, 1980).

Survivor guilt is a phenomenon that has appeared among the children too.

> Case: A thirteen-year-old son, while looking at pictures of his father's family, said: "I should not be here. His son should really be alive now. I am here because Hitler killed his son (Davidson)."

Nightmares and fright seem to be prevalent among children of survivors, though they were never in the camps.

> Case: A child of survivors, upon riding the subways in New York, has nightmares of trains going to Auschwitz.

These are some of the traumatic manifestations of the generational impact of the holocaust. The degree of disturbance varies with each individual according to family context and life experiences. Helping them to lead fuller lives is the overriding and challenging task of the professional.

### Treatment

There are several basic values in the treatment of survivors' children:

1.   The value of expressing feelings of anger toward parents, particularly the mother, in order to individuate from them.

2. The value of mourning for the dead and for lost youth in order to free oneself from the past.
3. In group therapy, the value of sharing and universalizing one's problems and receiving peer help.
4. In family therapy, the value of helping parents and children to express their feelings toward each other and to resolve the problem of separation—individuation.

The professional has several functions that bear explication because they are difficult to perform and they tend to create profound emotional responses. Fogelman and Savran (1980) describe these vividly and give case examples.

Professional responses to atrocity stories range from denial or intellectual and emotional distance, to overidentification. Denial still occurs, despite the abundant professional literature which should ideally enable therapists to face the issues and help clients to cope with them (Appelberg, 1972). Denial and intellectualization are functions of the anxiety of the professional who does not want to be the object of death fears.

Overidentification is a function of the immobilizing effect of the horror and the human degradation that evoke pity and compassion and reduce emotional distance between the professional and the client. Overidentification occurs more with the child than the parent. The professional sees the child as the *korban*—sacrifice—of the parents, and wants to give the child freedom and protection. He sees himself as the ideal parent (Klein, 1981).

One of the professional's major functions is to listen to the atrocity stories, despite the stress this evokes.

Cases: One of the group members reported that his father who had been in the gas chamber, had survived the initial trauma due to insufficient gas (p. 100).

Another member told the group that her father had to shovel corpses into the crematoria at Auschwitz (p. 101).

Fogelman and Savran (1980) report that the whole group, including themselves, the leaders, was stunned. Too shocked to ask how the others felt at hearing this, the group leaders were immobilized, for they became too deeply involved in the content of the discussion. This happens often in the countertransference, particularly when the leaders are themselves survivors' children.

The authors' self-revelation is a refreshing departure from the typical journal article which describes the survivors' symptoms and treatment, without including the conflicts, doubts, and errors of the therapist. For the therapist is human too and is prone to mistakes and failure with this population. As Gabriele Schiff (1980) states with regard to her work with survivors: "We also have to come to terms with the frustrating fact that in spite of our best intentions and well-developed skills, we will frequently fail (p. 314).

There were times in the survivor children's group when the client and the professional conspired to avoid disturbing issues. Perhaps the most difficult ones were the various stories of how their parents survived. The basic question was: what if our parents survived by compromising their morality? If the client is to be helped, he or she must be enabled to explore such unavoidable fantasies. Only when the fantasies are expressed can they be relinquished in the face of a known reality. The individual can then be freed of their disturbing presence.

Another professional function is the encouragement of public mourning in the group, such as crying.

> Case: When we cried along with group members, they felt freer to do the grieving they may have been ashamed of. We were not immune to crying when a child of survivors, who was also a child during the holocaust, shared his horrifying story of seeing his year-and-half old brother being thrown into a truck like a bundle of dirty laundry, with others piled one on top of the other (p. 101).

At a moment like this, it is more therapeutic physically to comfort or to cry along with the individual than to offer reflective comments. Crying shows the humanity of the professional, the lack of shame at this expression of empathy, and the falsity of the claim that professional distance is the hallmark of therapeutic effectiveness. When the client cries, as an expression of mourning, it can free him or her from the past, allay its gnawing anxieties, and thus enable the individual to function in the present. The laws of mourning in Judaism reflect these values and enable the mourner to return to normal functioning in society. Mourning in the therapeutic group is akin to the *shiva* observance in Judaism, where friends come to listen to the mourner verbalize the pain, guilt, and grief during the 7 days after the burial. By objectifying these feelings, the mourner is able to release them and to be freed from their psychic and emotional pressures.

Another function of the professional is the individualization of the client. In working with survivors and their children, populations whose symptoms have been widely described in the literature, the professional is apt to stereotype the client and not see the problems as they are actually manifested idiosyncratically in the individual's life. In addition, the attempt to individualize survivors' children must take into account their family constellation against the historical backdrop of the holocaust. The professional must be aware of the tensions that emanate from the interplay of the personal, familial, and historical forces in the life of the individual.

Survivor children are not always aware of the connection between their symptoms of malfunction and their parents' history. They tend to focus on their own life style, personality, and interpersonal relationships as the settings from which their difficulties arise. The professional's function in the process of collecting psychosocial data is intentionally to include family background and history. This vital information enables the

client to view him or herself in a biographical context in order
to examine more closely relationships with parents.

Schiff (1980), describing the professional's role with the
survivor, states:

> We have to admit that due to their experiences as well as
> those of their forebears, our clients can be annoying, exas-
> perating, and mentally unbalanced. It is understandable
> that we become impatient and frustrated, but we must not
> judge them morally; there are simply too many unknowns
> in the picture...We have to recognize that part of the
> survivor's mechanism of survival and dealing with guilt is
> to cling to his misery; try to take it away and we may get a
> complete breakdown (p. 314).

She suggests that some of the pain can be alleviated through lis-
tening, by pointing out that the client is not alone, by using
concrete services as a demonstration of caring, and by moving
with the client's pace and rhythm of development.

Hillel Klein (1981) suggests that empathy is the most
important attribute of the professional working with survivors'
children. The professional needs to facilitate the negative trans-
ference, and not to be the aggressor or the saviour but to feel
and mourn with them. The therapist should view the Survivor
Syndrome not as pathological, but as a positive strength in the
survivor's struggle against death.

What is the ultimate goal of working with survivors? The
professional cannot undo the damage that has been done, but
can only help the survivor to adjust to the existing realities.
This is really all that one can do for anyone who has gone
through any kind of tremendous trauma. The goal is to free the
survivor from the past in order to function in the present, and
to believe in the future.

What is the ultimate goal of working with survivors' children? To help them separate from their parents in order to
build and maintain satisfying social relationships and families
of their own—independence that is not rebellious and does not
exacerbate the sense of loss felt by their parents.

## Summary and Conclusions

The responsibilities of the professional working with holocaust survivors and their children are twofold: to help them develop and strengthen an orientation to the present via a confrontation with the haunting past; to prevent the generational effects from being transferred to the third and fourth generations.

These responsibilities must be translated into professional functions. Professionals need to be au courant with the literature on the faith and pathology of survivor families. To be effective in the use of themselves, they need to be aware of their own reactions to the holocaust, of its meaning to them as Jews, and of their own responses and interventions with clients. Professionals individualize their clients even as they view them in a familial and historical context; they show their feelings of compassion and empathy unabashedly and encourage clients to verbalize their pent-up feelings of anger, their fears, and fantasies. The professional stays in there, and does not flee from the terrible, the tragic, and the shameful.

Above all, the professional views survivors and their children as struggling with difficult human problems. Parents feel the need to assert their authority to "protect" their children from harm, and children strain for the freedom to become autonomous adults, unhaunted by their parents' past. The professional sees them as people with a great will to live, to raise children, and to be productive human beings in order to continue their family lineage and to build the Jewish future.

*Chapter 7*

# TOWARD A MODERN
# FAMILY PORTRAIT

In this book I have attempted to conceptualize and understand a complex phenomenon: the relationship between authority and autonomy as manifested in the Jewish family. While exploring the subject within the broader framework of tradition and modernity, I discovered that the four variables interpenetrated. Authority and tradition are closely related to each other, and both are intertwined with religion and widely considered to be irrational. Autonomy is a rational feature of modernity wherein institutions are challenged, choices abound, and the individual asserts him or herself with impunity.

Analysis of classical Judaic sources revealed that autonomy was sanctioned even in the presence of the centralized authority system—the Supreme Court. The scholar was permitted to assert his difference through the cogency of his argument, though he had to refrain from violating the court's decision in practice. The child was granted the autonomy to oppose his parents' restrictions on matters affecting his private life. In both institutions—the legal and the kinship—the rabbis sought to maintain a balance between conflicting interests and needs: on the one hand, the need to maintain order, stability, and continuity in the society and in one of its essential units, and on the other, the desire to protect and preserve the individual's intellectual integrity, and the satisfaction of personal needs. The rabbis' discussions reflect the tensions inherent in this dichotomy and the compromises that were necessary in order to achieve mutual satisfaction of conflicting interests.

The conflict between tradition and modernity poses similar issues for modern Jewish families who want to live in both worlds. These families do not want to be cut off from the tradition, but neither do they want to be insulated from modern society. Jewish families can be placed at many points along the continuum from tradition to modernity, depending on the degree to which they incorporate Jewish tradition into their acculturated life styles. Each struggles in its own way to negotiate the conflict and maintain viability as a Jewish family in a secular society.

There appears to be a positive correlation between tradition and authority, and modernity and autonomy. The modern Jewish family that is strongly identified with tradition tends to be more authoritarian in its child-rearing practices than the nontraditional family who, by being more closely identified with pluralism, tends to be more encouraging of children's autonomy. Nevertheless, there is a constant ideological tension that derives from each family's attempts to integrate Jewish values into its contemporary life style.

There are no panaceas and no programmatic shortcuts for resolving these problems of the modern Jewish family. This is due to the fact that the family, as an institution, interacts with all other institutions and is heavily influenced by them. Because it does not exist in a vacuum, the family experiences the stresses and strains that inhere in any social system where the whole is composed of interacting parts, and where changes in one affect the others. Parents and professionals are caught up in the maelstrom of social change, are confronted by challenges to all forms of authority, experimentation with alternate life styles, and negation of tradition as a viable guide for resolving value conflicts. Children are confused by the liberalization of choices in the society and the conservative tendencies of family living, i.e., the opportunities for self-determination vs. the commitment to traditional values. The generation gap is particularly wide today because of the influence of sociocultural change on traditional value systems.

It is, therefore, inevitable for parents to feel pangs of uncertainty regarding their lack of knowledge and their paucity of skills in raising children. This is especially so when chance, novelty, and the unexpected are major forces that affect families and professionals in ways that can neither be anticipated nor predicted. Parents and professionals feel the anguish of having to give up the Western notion that all problems can be solved. They develop instead an ability to live with unresolved problems. The essential questions are: How does one live with uncertainty? How does one become comfortable with the unknown (Setleis, 1980; Green, 1976)?

This chapter addresses these questions by drawing a portrait of the modern Jewish family in broad strokes. The portrait consists of an approach to tradition and modernity that enables Jewish families to function in the pluralistic situation, and helps professionals to tune in more keenly to their value conflicts.

## THE PARENTAL OUTLOOK

There are two aspects of family life that have particular meaning for parents who want to raise their children as Jews: tradition and purpose. Tradition refers to the beliefs, customs, mores, and rituals that have been forged together by Jews throughout their history to meet the requirements of daily living as a distinct group. The Jewish family today is part of the stream of Jewish tradition that emanates from the past and is constantly being recreated and reinterpreted in the present. "Tradition is a conserving device that savors the best in the experience of a people; it provides for the continuity of that experience with each generation's invigorating it with meaning as it is lived within that generation's reality (Setleis, p. 6)."

Each family develops its own traditions as members interact, argue, make up, and celebrate important events in their lives. Some traditions may be connected with Jewish events and others may not. Regardless of the unique nature of each family's traditions, there is an overarching Jewish tradition which Jewish families have deeply embedded in their consciousness over the milennia. This tradition has given the Jewish family its cohesiveness, purpose, and raison d'etre for raising children. It has provided the framework and structure for interaction and relationship. It has helped the family to resist the assimilationist forces of the larger society. It has served as the sacred canopy under which the family gained security in the course of raising its children as Jews.

The authority of this tradition is threatened by the forces of pluralism and by the ascendance of the private sphere as the arena for meaningful identity. What is needed is an approach that gives credibility to the intellectual heritage of Jewish tradition because it makes good sense to modern people, and not only because of nostalgic sentiment. The emphasis in this approach is not on the *Halakhah*, the requirement to conform to the details of Jewish law. The not-yet-committed Jewish family is not receptive to religious instruction on what is permissible and what is not. Such exhortations are effective only within a background of extensive Jewish education and commitment. Families with tenuous ties to Jewish learning and community would resist transforming their lives without an acceptable rationale, and would retain their option to choose among alternatives even in matters of faith and ritual. This approach respects the personal integrity of these families and reaches out to them where they are at. It accredits their desire to learn and to grow at their own pace. This approach, which is integrative, has educational, experiential, and social components. Educationally, it offers these families an opportunity to study the classical Judaic texts in their own language. This affords entry into the world of the text and the gaining of respect for the particular manner in which the Sages struggled with the problems of their day. The texts are then studied in the language of modern thought in order to make them comprehensible to the modern consciousness. Thus, the family is helped to translate the text from one language to another, and only then does it become intelligible and relevant.

The educational component needs to be buttressed by experience. Here, too, the teachers do not seek to impose their personal experiences and ritual forms on the learners. Their methods and skills are directed to assist the families to find their own way, to make intelligent, deliberate decisions regarding the Jewish way of life they wish to lead. They respect the integrity of the families and convey a belief in their ability to decide for themselves. This approach does not diminish the validity of the *Halakhah* but rather enhances it, for it encourages individuals and families to embrace it out of will and love and to enter into a dialogue with the tradition. Thus, Jewish behaviors are adopted out of conviction and not through coercion or habitualization. Their meanings enter conscious awareness through acts of will and do not disappear through the rote process. Awareness of the behavior, along with the knowledge of its underlying values, reinforces and enriches the experience.

The social component of this approach entails the integration of the educational and experiential in the communal setting. Individual families are apt to fail in this endeavor if they attempt to go it alone. Each family requires the reinforcement of other families in its search for Jewish significance. Consequently, many Jewish institutions including synagogues, federations, and community centers offer families the opportunity to experience Jewish life together in *havurot*—small groups—by praying, observing special holidays and events, studying together, making weekend retreats, trips to Israel, and sharing Shabbat and holiday meals.

The need for social contact and community is greater today than in earlier times as a result of the dispersion of extended families, the isolation of elderly parents in the inner cities, and the breaking up of old neighborhoods due to the changing demographic profiles of urban settings. Families are encouraged to reach out to other families to form small nuclei of concerned Jews who want to connect to Jewish tradition in serious ways.

The approach that has been proposed for not-yet-committed families applies equally to committed families. Despite their Jewish education and years of practicing Jewish behaviors, they, too, need to study classical Judaic texts with a modern vocabulary, for with each passing year, these texts can be interpreted differently due to changing circumstances and life experiences. These families should be encouraged to think in new ways and to question taken-for-granted Jewish beliefs and traditions. In this they have the support of Albo (cited in *Encyclopedia Judaica*, Vol. 7) who states: "It is clear now that every intelligent person is permitted to investigate the fundamental principles of religion and to interpret the biblical texts in accordance with the truth as it seems to him (p. 119)."

In the realm of the experiential, committed families also need to join with others—both committed and not-yet-committed—to study and observe Jewish celebrations in order to establish a feeling of community with the Jewish people. These activities have the effect of promoting social integration among families of all shades of religious observance.

With the integrative approach, the inevitable conflict between parental authority and child independence is no longer limited to their interpersonal relationship but becomes embedded in the larger encounter between tradition and modernity. The conflict is understood as a perennial issue in human and institutional development, with its resolution pointing toward a balance of mutual needs and interests. The framework of tradition and modernity provides the setting and the opportunity for families to clarify their values and purposes, define themselves in Jewish ways, and create Jewish experiences uniquely meaningful to all their members.

The serious questions that modern Jewish families must begin to ask themselves are: Which values should characterize our relationship as a family? What kind of adults do we want our children to be when they grow up? How should we relate to Jewish tradition? How do we live in the modern world and, at the same time, not cut ourselves off from the past? What are our purposes as a Jewish family?

Each family will need to struggle with these questions in its own way. Answers will not be easily forthcoming, nor will they be final. The quest for clarity of purpose is a continuous process for the family that negates the extreme options of insulation and assimilation and instead, chooses integration. The task of integrating the past with the present, traditional Jewish values with contemporary secular values, an ancient language with a modern language, requires serious attention and considerable effort. It encompasses educational, experiential, and social components that need to be fused if the family is to develop a vision of its future through a dialogue with the past.

## THE PROFESSIONAL OUTLOOK

Families who take the initiative to adopt the integrative option as their family model will evoke an enthusiastic response from professionals employed by the organized Jewish

community. But not all professionals are equipped to help
them pursue this goal. Many are wanting in Jewish education,
are unfamiliar with the language of the tradition, and do not
personally identify with the integrative option. Jewishness is a
taken-for-granted aspect of their predominantly secular lives,
and not a prominent feature of their consciousness. They affil-
iate with the Jewish community by being professionals. The
professional role permits many of them to be active, committed
Jews without having to have any sort of ideology. They solve
their Jewish problems by working for the Jews. The pattern
works so well that many lay people have learned to adopt it,
which is one of the reasons the Jewish federations succeed.
"Federations are veritable beehives of ideology-free Jewish
activity. People are asked to give money for the Jewish people,
and for Jewishness, without even having to ask why it is important for there to be Jewish people or a Jewish tradition (Israel,
1980, p. 307)."

However, there are many professionals who possess a
serious commitment to Jewish life which encompasses a
curiosity for Jewish learning, the practice of Jewish behaviors,
and a deep sense of belonging to the Jewish people. They are
equally committed to the viability of the Jewish family in its
struggle to preserve its difference from the larger society.

Families who want to develop a vision of their future may
need the professional's help in this undertaking. Is the
professional up to the task? Does he or she have a vision to set
before the family, against which they could clarify their own
stance? Green (1976) put the challenge to the professional
directly:

> What is your vision of the family as you sit around the
> table here tonight and plan to discuss the various types of
> programs that are being sponsored by your agencies? The
> social worker, the Jewish communal worker, cannot have
> a social policy which sets the principles and the objectives
> of family programming that help them decide the direc-
> tions in which they should go when there is no vision of

what the Jewish family should or might be. . . Let us put
our vision out, not as a covert idea, but as our model to
test what it is we are trying to do with the people we call
our members. Without such a model, without such a vision, agency planning for serving the Jewish family becomes meaningless (p. 4).

Professionals must work for a vision, not just an agency.
They must believe in something so strongly as to want to transform personal conviction into a life's work. They must try to
inject that vision into their work with families. This requires
that they have an ideology of the importance and meaning of
Jewish survival, that they feel free to express it in public, and
that they feel the pain of the gap between professing a belief
and translating it into practice. The integrative approach requires Jewish families to obtain a specialized Jewish education,
participate in Jewish experiences, and belong to Jewish social
groupings. Professionals will have to assist families to integrate
these endeavors.

To facilitate the intensive study of classical Judaic texts,
parents must be freed from some of their responsibilities by
staggered work hours, day care services, baby sitters, or bringing the classroom into the home. This learning requires the
organization of time and place with regularity, and a partial
restructuring of economic and social arrangements.

Maximizing the educational effort requires the meticulous
preparation of texts on central themes in Jewish thought,
accompanied by probing questions for discussion. These mate-
rials could take the form of pamphlets on selected subjects
which may also include classical sources in philosophy, political
and social science, and psychology.

In the actual teaching process, participants are encouraged to think for themselves, to come up with their own interpretations of the texts, and to offer their insights based on
their intellectual grasp and life experiences. Everyone's contribution has value. The teacher encourages continuous probing
to enhance the variety and depth of interpretations.

Along with Jewish study, the professional and the agency offer families the opportunity to experience different aspects of Judaism by living them *in actu*: the Shabbat, festivals, memorial observances, prayer, rites of passage, giving *tzedakah*, and visiting Israel. These experiences are given new dimensions of meaning when families participate selectively in the ancient rituals based on their readiness, adapt them and contribute their own interpretation, and use their own vocabulary to achieve understanding. The professional is urged to exercise self-restraint in the temptation to impose his or her own ritual forms onto their experiences: the professional realizes that they are trying to find their way, and the task is to help them by offering knowledge, expertise, and options.

The social dimension refers to the creation of a sense of belonging to a community. It is intertwined with the educational and the experiential, for textual study and cultural experiences take place in groups. The community that is formed is a new community of the Jewish spirit, consisting of a group of people who meet and share in order to deepen their Jewish identities and visions. It transcends geographic boundaries and agency memberships. The call goes out to all Jewish families in the area—extended families, nuclear families, single-parent families, intermarried families, reconstituted families, nonaffiliated families, and singles, to create their Jewish future by committing themselves to study and practice together, and in the privacy of their own homes.

The professional's own zeal must be communicated if he or she is to ignite a spark of enthusiasm for this project. Truly valuing Jewish families and believing in the possibility of their growth, the professional will serve them with dedication and specialized skills to help them translate their visions into reality. The ideal is achieved when the entire community dedicates itself to an active, formal quest for meaningful Jewish living.

This book has presented one person's vision of what the modern Jewish family can become—a social unit which retains generational differences, where children learn such fundamentals of human relationships as love, interdependence, and respect for elders, and where parents and children respect each others' needs for authority and independence. Parent-child interaction is conceived in the broader framework of the interaction between tradition and modernity. Jewish tradition is to be understood in pluralistic terms, available for the individual to grasp on the intellectual and experiential level. Each family member is encouraged to relate to Jewish tradition according to one's own level of comprehension. As the family translates the tradition into the language it understands, the tradition becomes a life force that guides the family in the resolution of its value conflicts and in its planning for the future.

## REFERENCES

Abarbanel, I. *Commentary on the Torah* (Heb.) Jerusalem: Torah V'daath, 1956.

Adler, B. *Halakhot Va—Halikhot Bar-Mitzvah* (Heb.) Jerusalem: Feldheim, 1977.

Appelberg, Esther. Holocaust survivors and their children. In N. Linzer (Ed.), *The Jewish Family*. New York: Federation of Jewish Philanthropies, 1972.

Arendt, H. *Between Past and Future*. New York: Meridian Books, 1966.

*Babylonian Talmud*. I. Epstein, (Ed. and trans.) London: Soncino Press, 1960.

Becker, E. *The Denial of Death*. New York: Free Press, 1973.

Benedict, R. *Patterns of Culture*. New York: New American Library, 1954.

Berger, P.L. *Facing up to Modernity: Excursions in Society, Politics and Religion*. New York: Basic Books, 1977.

Berger, P.L. *The Heretical Imperative*. New York: Doubleday, 1979.

Berger, P.L. *The Sacred Canopy*. New York: Doubleday, 1968.

Berger, P.L., & Luckmann, T. *The Social Construction of Reality*. New York: Doubleday, 1967.

Bernstein, S. Self-determination: King or citizen in the realm of values? *Social Work*, 1960, *5* (1), 3-8.

Bialik, H.N., & Rabinitzky, Y.C. (Eds.) *Sefer Ha-Aggadah* (Heb.) Tel Aviv: Dvir, 1960.

Blidstein, G. *Honor Thy Father and Mother: Filial Responsibility in Jewish Law and Ethics*. New York: Ktav, 1975.

Blos, P. *On Adolescence*. New York: Free Press, 1962.

Brenner, R.R. *The Faith and Doubt of Holocaust Survivors*. New York: Free Press, 1980.

Brown, J.K. Adolescent initiation rites among preliterate peoples. In R.E. Grinder (Ed.) *Studies in Adolescence*. New York: Macmillan, 1963.

Buber, M. *Eclipse of God: Studies in the Relation Between Religion and Philosophy*. New York: Harper & Sons, 1952.

Burgess, E.W., Locke, H.J., & Thomas, M.M. *The Family: From Institution to Companionship* (3rd ed.). New York: American Book Co., 1963.

Carrilio, T.E. Testing a theory of the borderline-narcissistic personality. *Social Work*, 1981, *26* (2), 107–112.

*Celebrating the Jewish Holy Days*. Jerusalem: Shalom Hartman Institute, 1980.

Clements, R.E. *Cambridge Bible Commentary*. Cambridge: Cambridge University Press, 1972.

Davidson, S. The clinical effects of massive psychic trauma in families of holocaust survivors. *Journal of Marital and Family Therapy*, 1980, *6* (1) 11–22.

Eliot, T.S. *Selected Essays*. London: Faber & Faber, 1963.

*Encyclopedia Judaica*. Jerusalem: Keter Publishing, 1972.

Erikson, E.H. *Childhood and Society*. New York: W.W. Norton, 1950.

Erikson, E.H. Youth: Fidelity and diversity. In E.H. Erikson (Ed.), *Youth: Change and Challenge*. New York: Basic Books, 1963.

*The Evil Impulse: A Study Guide*. Jerusalem: Shalom Hartman Institute, 1980.

Fogelman, E., & Savran, B. Brief group therapy with off-spring of holocaust survivors: Leaders' reactions. *American Journal of Orthopsychiatry*, 1980, *50* (1) 96–108.

Friedrich, Carl. *Tradition and Authority.* London: Macmillan, 1972.

Freyberg, J.T. Difficulties in separation-individuation as experienced by offspring of Nazi holocaust survivors. *American Journal of Orthopsychiatry*, 1980, *50*, (1) 87–95.

Green, S.H. The Jewish family. New York: Wurzweiler School of Social Work, Yeshiva University, 1976 (mimeographed).

Hartman, D. *Jewish Values: Implications for Jewish Federations.* Jerusalem: Shalom Hartman Institute, 1978.

Hartman, D. *Joy and Responsibility.* Jerusalem: Ben-Zvi-Posner, 1978.

Hartman, D. *Maimonides: Torah and Philosophic Quest.* Philadelphia: Jewish Publication Society, 1976.

Heschel, A.J. *The Insecurity of Freedom.* New York: Farrar, Straus and Giroux, 1967.

Hirsch, S.R. *The Pentateuch.* (I. Levy trans. & exp.) London: Isaac Levy, 1963.

Hirsch, S.R. *The Hirsch Siddur.* New York: Feldheim, 1969.

*The Holy Scriptures.* Jerusalem: Koren Publishers, 1977.

*Israel: A study guide.* Jerusalem: Shalom Hartman Institute, 1980.

Israel, R.J. The challenge of outreach: Turning on turned-off Jews. *Journal of Jewish Communal Service*, 1980, *56* (4) 306–309.

Jastrow, M. *A Dictionary of the Targumim, the Talmud Babli and Yerushalmi and the Midrashic Literature.* (2 vol.) New York: Pardes Publishing Co., 1950.

The Jerusalem Seminar Series of the Shalom Hartman Institute, *Shefa*, 1980, 2 (2) 85-6.

Kaufman, Y. Coercion and freedom in education. In *Encyclopedia of Education* (Heb.) (Vol. 1). Jerusalem: Bialik Institute, 1961, 714.

Keith-Lucas, A. A critique of the principle of self-determination. *Social Work*, 1963, 8 (2) 66-71.

Keniston, K. Social change and youth in America. In E.H. Erikson, (Ed.). *Youth: Change and Challenge*. New York: Basic Books, 1963.

Kestenberg, J.S. Psychoanalytic contributions to the problem of children of survivors from Nazi persecution. *The Israel Annals of Psychiatry and Related Disciplines*, 1972, *10* (4) 311-325.

Klein, H. Address before Israel Medical Association. Jerusalem: March, 1981.

Kolitz, Z. Yossel Rakover's appeal to God. In A.H. Friedlander, (Ed.), *From Out of the Whirlwind: A Reader of Holocaust Literature*. New York: Union of American Hebrew Congregations, 1968.

Kook, A. *Olat Reiyah* (Heb.) (2 vol.), Jerusalem: Mossad Harav Kook, 1963.

Krystal, H. (Ed.), *Massive Psychic Trauma*. New York: International Universities Press, 1968.

Lang, J. The changing Jewish family and the crisis of values: The role and impact of the professional in Jewish communal service. *Journal of Jewish Communal Service*, 1980, *56* (4), 301-305.

Lasch, C. *The Culture of Narcissism*. New York: W.W. Norton, 1978.

Levine, B. *Some Notes on the Good and Evil Inclinations*. Jerusalem: Shalom Hartman Institute, 1981.

Lidz, T. *The Person*. New York: Basic Books, 1976.

Linzer, N. *The Jewish Family*. New York: Federation of Jewish Philanthropies, 1972.

Linzer, N. *The Nature of Man in Judaism and Social Work*. New York: Federation of Jewish Philanthropies, 1978.

Maimonides, M. *Commentary to the Mishnah*. (J. Kafih, trans.) Jerusalem: Mossad Harav Kook, 1963.

Maimonides, M. *Mishneh Torah* (Heb.) Jerusalem: Mossad Harav Kook, 1956.

Maimonides, M. *Sefer Ha-Mitzvot*. (Heb.) New York: Rabbi Leib Reinman, 1955.

Marx, T. *Authority and Independence in Parent-Child Relationships*. (Heb.). Jerusalem: Shalom Hartman Institute, 1980.

Mead, M. *Coming of Age in Samoa*. New York: New American Library, 1956.

Neiderland, W. Address at Grief and Bereavement Conference, Yeshiva University, October, 1977.

Newman, L. Emotional disturbance in children of holocaust survivors. *Social Casework*, 1979, *60* (1) 43–50.

Ostow, M. The determinants of Jewish identity: A maturational approach. In *Issues in Jewish Identity*. New York: American Jewish Committee, 1977.

Perlman, H. H. "Self-Determination: Reality or illusion?" *Social Service Review*, 1965, *39* (4), 410–421.

Poll, S. *The Hasidic Community of Williamsburg*. New York: Schocken, 1969.

Popper, K. *Conjectures and Refutations: The Growth of Scientific Knowledge*. New York: Harper, 1965.

*Purim: A Study Guide*. Jerusalem: Shalom Hartman Institute, 1980.

Reiner, B. A feeling of irrelevance: The effects of a nonsupportive society. *Social Casework*, 1979, *60* (1), 3–10.

Rogers, C. *Client-centered Therapy.* London: Constable, 1976.

Rubinstein, R. *After Auschwitz: Radical Theology and Contemporary Judaism.* Indianapolis: Bobbs-Merrill, 1966.

Rubinstein, R. Homeland and holocaust. In D.R. Cutler, (Ed.) *The Religious Situation.* Boston: Beacon Press, 1968.

Setleis, L. The Jewish communal worker confronts Jewish family values. *Jewish Social Work Forum,* 1981, *17,* 1 – 9.

Setleis, L. The struggle to believe: An institutional crisis. *Confrontation,* 1979, *18,* 147 – 152.

Schachter, Z. Commentary on Rubinstein. In D. R. Cutler, (Ed.) *The Religious Situation.* Boston: Beacon Press, 1968.

Schiff, G. The legacy of displaced persons—a personal chronicle. *Journal of Jewish Communal Service,* 1980, *56* (4), 310 – 315.

Schneider, S. Attitudes toward death in adolescent offspring of holocaust survivors. *Adolescence,* 1978, *13* (52), 575 – 584.

Schwartz, W. Between client and system: The mediating function. In R. W. Roberts, & H. Northen, (Eds.) *Theories of Social Work with Groups.* New York: Columbia University Press, 1976.

Seeley, J. R., Sim, R. A., & Loosley, E. W. *Crestwood Heights.* New York: Basic Books, 1956.

Shils, E. *Tradition.* Chicago: University of Chicago Press, 1981.

*Shulkhan Arukh-* Code of Jewish Law.

Sklare, M., & Greenblum, J. *Jewish Identity on the Suburban Frontier.* New York: Basic Books, 1968.

Soloveitchik, J. B. Catharsis. *Tradition,* 1978, 17 (2) 38 – 54.

Soloveitchik, J. B. The community. *Tradition, 1978, 17 (2)* 7 – 24.

Soloveitchik, J. B. The lonely man of faith. *Tradition, 1965, 7* (2) 3 – 65.

Strean, H. The contemporary family and the responsibilities of the social worker in direct practice. *Journal of Jewish Communal Service,* 1979, 56 (1) 40 – 49.

Tuteur, W. One hundred concentration camp survivors: Twenty years later. *Israel Annals of Psychiatry,* 1966, *4* (1) 78-90.

Uryan, M. Fathers and children in hasidism. In M. Hovev (Ed.) *Jewish Families* (Heb.) Jerusalem: Torah Culture Department, 1976.

Weber, M. *The Theory of Social and Economic Organization* ( A. M. Henderson & T. Parsons, Eds. and trans.) New York: Oxford, 1947.

Weisel, E. *Night.* New York: Hill & Wang, 1960.

Weisel, E. *Gates of the Forest.* New York: Avon, 1969.

Weisel, E. Jewish values in the post-holocaust future. *Judaism,* 1967, *16* (3) 281-284.

Winnik, H. Z. Further comments concerning problems of late pathological effects of Nazi persecution and their therapy. *Israel Annals of Psychiatry,* 1967, *5* (1) 1-16.

Zborowski, M. & Herzog, E. *Life is with People.* New York: Schocken, 1967.

# INDEX